BECAUSE OUR FATHERS LIED

Death and Deception Afloat and Ashore

J. F. Leahy

NAVAL
WRITERS GROUP
HONOR, COURAGE, COMMITMENT

If any question why we died,
Tell them, because our fathers lied.

Epitaphs of the War
Rudyard Kipling
1914-1918

AUTHOR'S NOTES:

This is a work of fiction: While much of this narrative relates events precisely as they are recorded by contemporaneous accounts or in scholarly research, other significant elements of this story are solely products of the author's imagination. References and sources may be found at the rear of this volume. It is often said that truth is stranger than fiction. I leave it to the wisdom of the reader to discern between the two.

Although writing has been described as the loneliest of professions, no book is solely the work of the author listed on the cover. It is said that no man is a hero to his valet; neither is an author to his editor, particularly an author whose understanding of the rules of punctuation is as tentative as mine. I am grateful to Ms. Carolyn Dinovo for once again rescuing me from the results of my indolence in the third grade. Boxes of gently used commas will soon appear on Ebay. Thank Carolyn!

A glossary of nautical usage and other terms which may be unfamiliar to the general reader is located at the end of this narrative.

TABLE OF CONTENTS

CHAPTER 1
GIVE PEACE A CHANCE

Becky Franks and Doctor Hans Vlanderen (*Wandering Hands*, to the nurses assigned to his rotation) waited impatiently in the basement of the *Blind Boatman* Jazz club. The *Blind Boatman* was a dilapidated former row house on Sansom Street in Philadelphia near the University of Pennsylvania's campus, and housed a progressive book shop on the first floor and a stuffy coffeehouse in the basement. It was a favorite meeting place for students and others who opposed the war in Vietnam. Becky and the doctor had dated intermittently, depending on their schedules at University Hospital, and the nurse and first-year resident shared deeply-held pacifist beliefs. Becky's dad had been lost at sea in 1941; Hans had suffered hunger and severe deprivation in war-torn Rotterdam. Both traumas informed their lives and beliefs.

"Becky, has anyone heard from Joel? He was supposed to be here an hour ago."

"It's not like him to be late. I heard that there is some problem at SEPTA's 40th St. subway portal; maybe he's stuck in traffic."

Joel Staghorn, a slight, bespectacled graduate student, whose tightly curled black hair was usually in disarray, was the charismatic leader of

1

Pacifists Against Vietnam Escalation (PAVE), and in recent months had emerged as a leader among the many aniti-war protest groups at the university.

Joel was usually accompanied by an audience of like-minded supporters, most of whom were driven by opposition to the injustices of America's actions in a war 12,000 miles away. As the the youngest son of a dentist and a school psychologist who grew up in the solidly middle-class Mayfair neighborhood of the city, he was an unlikely leader of the protest movement. His older brother had served as a lieutenant in the army's Finance Corps and had recently returned, disillusioned, from a tour of duty in Saigon. Joel's associates enjoyed his sharp sense of humor which many of the young female undergraduates found irresistible. He had been one of the primary organizers of *PAVE,* an acronym which he felt to be particularly appropriate and pleasing.

After a few more minutes, the door to the *Blind Boatman* swung open and Joel Staghorn, dripping wet, arrived.

"Man, it's a mess out there. It's pouring rain, and when we got to 40th Street, two of the subway-surface cars had collided, blocking the eastbound track. I waited for about twenty-five minutes and then got off and walked the rest of the way. I feel like a drowned rat."

"There's been nothing but rain this whole summer," remarked Sarah Kaufman, a straggly- haired, angular freshman from St. Louis, with a face like a plateful of mortal sins. She had been attracted to the antiwar movement, and to Joel in particular. Accompanying her was Murray Sherman, whose parents were funding his education in accounting ; a career which the brash and bespectacled young man with a wispy goatee and wild Afro hairstyle found particularly distasteful. A Long Island native, he found his recent friendship with Sarah to be one of the greatest accomplishments of his young and unremarkable life.

2

The last to arrive was one "Susan Sparkles" (nee Mary Catherine O' Riley, formerly of the decidedly working class neighborhood of Manayunk.) She had wandered into the *Blind Boatmen* one freezing afternoon several months previously, ostensibly just to get warm. She had struck up a conversation with Staghorn, who quickly began fantasizing that this energetic young lady had some personal attraction to him. She most certainly did, but not of the erotic type which Staghorn had assumed. She quickly evolved into his "Girl Friday", and became responsible for all communication, both internal and external, having to do with the movement. When Susan entered she untucked a brown steno pad from beneath her peasant blouse and tie-dyed jeans, where she had placed it to keep it dry from the rain outside, and greeted everyone at the table and sat quietly by Joel's side in the now crowded cellar.

"Ah," said Joel, "It looks like were all here now. Does anyone have anything new to report?"

"There are posters all over campus calling for a march on Independence Hall on the Fourth of July," Susan reported. "It looks like SDS (Students for a Democratic Society) is taking the lead on this, but the Campaign for Nuclear Disarmament, the Central Committee for Conscientious Objectors, and the Anarchist's Commune also have a role in organizing it. More troubling, I heard someone say that the Black Panthers are going to march in solidarity with everyone. Is this something we might want to do?" she asked.

"Well it will certainly bring attention and a lot of good publicity to us if we decide to join the march." replied Joel. "I'm not worried about the Central Committee or the nuclear disarmament people, but things could get hairy if the Anarchists and the Panthers are there. We will have to wait and see, I suppose."

"I believe you've all seen the news about what's happening in the Delta this week," Murray interjected. "It's the same old shit. Our soldiers and the ARVN are raping and killing women and children and no one seems to give a damn. We've been cutting off the ears and abusing the bodies of peasant farmers who we've been shooting from our helicopters, and all these poor Vietnamese want to do is to work safely in their rice paddies. We are playing right into the Viet Cong's hands; every time we kill a suspected 'guerrilla' we make three more out of people who might have otherwise been our friends and allies. And the kids who are being drafted now are being indoctrinated that these people are somehow the enemies of freedom and democracy and that the 'Domino Effect,' whatever the hell that means, poses some sort of imminent danger to America."

"But what about the threat that insurrection poses to America's interests?" asked Dr. Vlanderen.

"There is nothing that happens in Southeast Asia that could ever threaten America in my view," Murray replied, "Yet politicians like LBJ, Nixon, and three quarters of Congress want to keep sending more troops, more napalm, more warplanes and aircraft carriers, so that we can bomb them back into the Stone Age, as General Westmoreland said recently. Hell, these poor people want nothing to do with us; they would just like us to go home. They want us to leave them alone, and they survived by aligning themselves with whoever is winning this crazy war, be it the North Vietnamese Army, the Viet Cong or, even on some rare occasions, us. And the American people don't really care, unless they have a family member who's been sucked into this madness. You can walk away from this campus and within a quarter of a mile you'll find thousands of people who don't have a clue as to what's happening and, unless they have someone there, don't much care. All they would rather do down in South Philly or Roxborough or up in the Northeast is to sit and watch Bonanza or the Beverly Hillbillies at night. About the only time they ever see a soldier or Marine, most of them, is on Gomer Pyle."

"You're right, of course," Joel replied. Even Walter Cronkite, 'the most trusted man in America,' got it right a couple months ago when he ended his broadcast by saying:

'Who won and who lost in the great Tet offensive against the cities? I'm not sure. The Vietcong did not win by a knockout, but neither did we. The referees of history may make it a draw. It seems now more certain than ever that the bloody experience of Vietnam is to end in a stalemate. But it is increasingly clear to this reporter that the only rational way out then will be to negotiate, not as victors, but as honorable people who lived up to their pledge to defend democracy, and did the best they could.'

His companions murmured their ascent, as Susan scribbled in her steno pad.

Joel thought aloud. "Well, if we get involved in this Fourth of July march we may hammer home this message where it hurts the most. These reactionaries think that the Fourth of July is somehow a sacred holiday dedicated to celebrating life, liberty, and the pursuit of happiness. This might be an opportunity to show them differently if we were to march on Independence Hall. If we can be sure that it will stay non-violent we can show everyone in the city that we're not just pointy-headed liberal academics over here at Penn."

"Susan, let's get some fliers mimeographed using our name, and then let's check with the other groups to determine who the key people are that will be organizing and acting as stewards for the march. I promise you though, if the Panthers are taking any kind of a leadership role, we ought to sit this one out. But I imagine by the weekend we can post the fliers throughout the campus and we may be able to rally more students to our pacifistic point of view."

Becky raised another point. "Joel, do you think that we ought to apply for a permit ourselves to march separately to Independence Hall?"

"Well, we're not the lead organizers here. I don't want us to look like the little kids who run along the sidewalks waving their flags as the parade goes down the street. I'll leave that up to the main organizers. Although, personally, I don't think we should need a permit to walk the streets of any city in this country."

"I'm certain the police will be there," Murray interjected.

"No doubt. But if they try to stop it they'll just be playing into everyone's hands. It will show them up and everyone will see what freedom and democracy means in this City of Brotherly Love. As repressive as the police department has become since the Columbia Avenue disturbances a few years back, I don't think they would be so reckless as to allow a police riot on July 4th on the lawn of the cradle of democracy."

Joel and Susan posted fliers throughout the campus over the next several days in support of the rally, while Becky and Sarah designed and printed placards and banners for the march. Joel enthusiastically approved the slogan "PAVE the Way to Peace in Vietnam" and the general consensus was that this should be a fairly risk-free opportunity. Some of the more radical protesters on campus, however, thought that Staghorn and his small group of pacifists would be the perfect stooges to deflect attention from their more sinister agendas. Word spread very quickly through the underground movements that the fireworks on this Fourth of July should not be missed.

Anti-war protest march, Philadelphia, Spring 1968

CHAPTER 2
THE THIN BLUE LINE

Monday, June 24, 1968 - Philadelphia

The commissioner savored his coffee quietly as he gazed out the windows of his third floor office at the Roundhouse, the police administration building at 8th and Race Streets, just east of Philadelphia's Chinatown. His long serving secretary, Helen Valli, busied herself arranging the office for the day's business. "I'll tell you, Helen; this job is a long way from walking a beat in the 39th district. When I first got up there, as a rookie right out of the police academy, that fat Irish desk sergeant took one look at me and asked me if I was the new dago assigned to the district. I told him if I heard that word from him again, I'd knock him flat on his ass. So I spent the next six months on last-out, patrolling Laurel Hill Cemetery from midnight to 8 AM. Every day I'd go home and my father, a police officer himself for 25 years, would ask me how the shift went. And every time he heard the same answer: "Pretty dead."

Miss Valli, used to the commissioner's well known candor (a police reporter once remarked, "Ah, Frank would say Mass if he only remembered the Latin"), laughed softly. She'd heard that story, or variations of it, dozens of times.

He looked out the window at the city of Camden, across the river in New Jersey.

"You know, Helen, I don't know what this country is headed, but it's a pretty good chance that wherever the hell we're going, Camden will get there first." She laughed more openly, and glanced at the large office clock on the far wall.

"Just a reminder, Commissioner, you have a meeting at 9:00. I've got the whole list here and as soon as the last one arrives I'll bring them in. You've got a pretty large group today: both deputy commissioners, the central division and tactical division inspectors, a couple captains and lieutenants and one lonely sergeant coming.

"We can fit them around my conference table, Helen. That lonely sergeant may be the most important guy at the meeting. That's George Pencil, the head of the Civil Disobedience Squad. With all these radical hippies and troublemakers marching around, he's the busiest guy in the city nowadays."

The commissioner finished his coffee, and turned his attention to the fresh copies of the *Philadelphia Inquirer* which Helen had placed on his desk before his arrival. The world was in turmoil and it looked as if a long, hot summer in Philadelphia was a certainty. A few months earlier, Lyndon B. Johnson had announced that he would not run for reelection, and Gene McCarthy and the usual cast of Democrats were scurrying around in an attempt to win the nomination. "I always liked the *first* Senator McCarthy better," he thought. Things were more stately on the Republican side; Nixon appeared to have a lock on the nomination. The country was divided over Vietnam and it was only a matter of time before it exploded, not only in Philadelphia but throughout the nation, he mused.

Helen returned. "Are you about ready for the meeting?" He nodded. As the attendees entered they stood in deference until "The Boss" took his seat at the head of the large, oval-shaped table. Present were the brass hats as well as Captains Tony Chen, sixth district commander (Center City-East),

Captain Ken Davis of the ninth district (Center City-West), and Captain Al Davis of the eighteenth district, which surrounded the Campus of the University of Pennsylvania. Also present were Lieutenants Leon Dexter of the Traffic Bureau, Thomas "Doc" Holiday of the elite Highway Patrol and Tony Markle of the Stakeout unit, as well as Sgt. Pencil of the Civil Disobedience Squad. After a few minutes of pleasantries and departmental gossip he brought the meeting to order. "Sgt. Pencil, I believe you have something to discuss with us?"

"I do, Commissioner. As you know, we've been monitoring a number of dissident groups including several that infest the Penn campus. One group in particular, PAVE (Pacifists Against Vietnam Escalation), is relatively new here in town, but we suspect links to well-known anarchist groups in Washington and in New York. The local group seems to take its marching orders from a 24-year old hippie named Joel Staghorn. As dissidents go, he is minor league, but it looks like he's aiming to become a voice in the anti-Vietnam war movement. We have a couple of good sources inside his organization: one is a medical resident at University Hospital who we were able to turn when we found a small quantity of drugs he pilfered from the hospital pharmacy during a car stop up in Tacony. The other is the wife of a young rookie up in the fifth District in Roxborough. Her father actually retired from the thirteenth district, back when it was on Main Street in Manayunk. She came to us and volunteered her services in return for a spot in the next academy class. She acts as a go-fer for Staghorn's group and is a very good source of information concerning his plans. Both of them confirmed to us that Staghorn and PAVE are planning a march from the Penn campus to Independence Hall on the morning of July 4. From the looks of it, he's coordinating with SDS, the Worker's Party, and a whole group of others to make this a major event. We think that he may have over 8000 marchers lined up, many of whom have documented records of violence, both in the Columbia Avenue riots a couple years ago and elsewhere. We're considering this a major threat."

"Thank you George, that's why I asked all of you to get together with me this morning. I've heard similar rumblings from City Hall, and when I talked to Mayor Tate yesterday, he himself was concerned. The last thing he wants is a violent demonstration with Independence Hall as a scenic backdrop. The issue as he sees it is for us to keep these bozos contained, allow them to march peacefully with their bullhorns and signs through the heart of Center City, and yet keep close control on where they're going and what they're doing."

"Captain Chen, this one looks like it's going to be mostly on you. Together with the guys in the 9th and the 18th, you'll need to keep these people as closely contained as you can. If they're coming off the Penn campus, we can herd them down Walnut Street, and across the bridge and through Rittenhouse Square. We'll let them chant and scream and do their thing in the square, and we'll tip off the TV people so they can get shots for their newscasts. That should entertain the liberals and do-gooders in the neighboring penthouses. After that we'll let them swing up 18th street to Chestnut, turn right on Chestnut and then down to Independence Hall. Tony, have you had a chance to get with John O'Mera of the US Park Service police detachment at Independence Hall?"

"I haven't yet, Boss, but I will before the day is out. He may want to bring in some extra personnel from other locations. I suspect both the Washington DC Park Service police and the guys at the Statue of Liberty in New York are going to be pretty busy, but he may be able to get some additional help from Valley Forge or Gettysburg."

"Well, that's I would do if I were in his position. Al, have you had a chance to talk with that new guy Worthington that took over the University of Pennsylvania police?"

"That guy is a real piece of work in my opinion, sir. He's got no law enforcement experience whatsoever. He used to be a professor of law up at

John Jay College in New York, and he's totally at the beck and call of the Faculty Senate since he arrived here in Philly. And most of them in my opinion are commies or commie sympathizers. They do have a long history on that campus of not only tolerating, but actively encouraging civil disobedience."

"Yeah, I've hear that egghead Worthington couldn't track a bleeding elephant in a snowstorm," the Commissioner chuckled. "He hasn't even had the decency to schedule a courtesy call with me. I hope he's not waiting for me to appear on the Penn campus, because the only way I'm going over there is to lead a charge of Highway guys right up the front steps of College Hall. With all this antiwar sentiment, half of those jackass professors will just use this 'peaceful demonstration' as a pretext for a good riot. Hell, I'm against this damn war, too. Anybody with any sense is. Meanwhile all these rich SOBs at Penn are burning up daddy's money out destroying property and disturbing the peace. I told Tate when I saw him that we should come down hard, but of course Tate is terrified of destroying our image with the tourist trade."

"Anyway, here's what I want you guys to do. Tony, this thing is going to go through your district one way or another. Make damn sure you have enough guys to cover the entire route, and pay particular attention to the major department stores along Chestnut Street. These anarchists would just love to break a couple of display windows on the way to their protest. Kenny, set up your guys in the Ninth as a blocking force in case any of those Temple University radicals start heading down Broad Street to connect with the main march. I don't think you're going to have a lot of trouble up there; they know what happened to them on Columbia Avenue the last time they got antsy, back in '64. But you never know, and it's better to be prepared than sorry."

"Leon, I want you to make sure that these people keep on the Walnut Street route until we get them up to Chestnut Street and we don't have

13

any strays wandering around. Tell the Fairmount Park Guards I want to 'borrow' their mounted unit, and have all your motorcycle patrols working at the side streets as well. The horses will help keep things under control."

"Doc, I want everybody from Highway working this event. We'll use your guys as a reaction force in case things get hairier than we expect. Maybe you'd want to split your group into two sections, one concentrating on Rittenhouse Square and the other one backing up the National Park Service guys down at Independence Hall. There is nothing like a bunch of guys with boots and batons to make believers out of anybody."

"Tony Markle, I'd like to have your stakeout guys in plainclothes all around the march route. You all can weigh in if things get ugly. In the meantime you can be judging the sentiments and intentions of the bystanders. Personally, I think we have enough firepower that we could invade Cuba if we wanted to and still keep the mayor happy that all the mommies and daddies who are bringing little Joey and Janie to see the Liberty Bell are not unduly affected. As for me, I was planning on going down the shore for the Fourth of July, and I still might; I'll keep my options open though, depending on what more we learn about these radicals. You guys got that? We've got about ten days until the holiday."

"Sgt. Pencil, I want your guys to keep a very close eye on this and keep me informed. And all of you – the one thing we are *not* going to do is to get the State Police involved in any of this. If I get any word that those morons at the Belmont Barracks are sticking their noses in, I swear I'll go out there myself and arrest their troop commander. This is our police force and our city and we'll take care of things our way, understood? Let's meet again at the same time next Monday, or sooner if George has vital information, and we'll see where we are."

Frank Rizzo, Commissioner, Police Department of Philadelphia in 1968

CHAPTER 3
DOWN TO THE SEA IN SHIPS

Thursday, July 4, 1968 - Delaware River

Captain Tom Carpentier was tired. He was approaching the end of his six-month rotation as master of the *SS Rita Elizabeth Sykes*, and had just completed a routine North Atlantic passage from Antwerp to Brooklyn, NY. The *Rita Elizabeth Sykes*, like all ships of the Sykes Brothers Shipping Company, was named after a member of the prominent Louisiana shipping family, in this case the late mother of Terrence P. Sykes, former president and current chairman of the board. Laid down at Cramp's Shipbuilding Company in Philadelphia's Port Richmond section in November 1941 and launched in March 1942, the war-weary vessel had seen service in both the Atlantic and Pacific theaters during World War II. A general dry-cargo ship (break bulk) it displaced 14,000 tons, with a length of 460 feet and a beam of 64 feet. It drew 24 feet 6 inches when load to its summer Plimsoll line and her single shaft 6000 hp steam propulsion plant was capable of 16 knots in calm seas.

Sailing essentially in ballast, with only a light load of household goods and personal automobiles shipped by re-deploying military personnel in Europe, the *Rita E* (as the ship was fondly nicknamed by a generation of NMU mariners) was forced to anchor-out in Upper New York Bay while awaiting an open berth at the Red Hook Marine Terminal. Moreover, when she later attempted to raise steam to depart Brooklyn, she suffered a casualty to her main condenser and was forced to remain for repairs for three additional days. When she finally set sail for Philadelphia and Baltimore, she was at least 72 hours behind the schedule set for her by the Military Sea Transportation Service to which she was chartered.

Nevertheless, as she rounded Sandy Hook and turned south for Philadelphia she was running well, and Captain Carpentier hoped that she would make up the time en route, and that the Sykes agents had made appropriate arrangements for a quick load-and-go along the Delaware River. She was scheduled to pick up military materials destined for the war zone in Southeast Asia, and after taking the ship through the Delaware and Chesapeake Canal to Locust Point in Baltimore, Captain Carpentier was scheduled to be relieved and was looking forward to spending the next several months on shore leave.

Sailing south, at about 14 knots to avoid unnecessary strain on the aging power plant, the *Rita E.* was abeam the Cape Henlopen pilot station shortly before 2100 on the evening of Wednesday, July 3rd. As the Lewes, Delaware pilot stepped aboard, Captain Tom exchanged pleasantries and learned that high water at Philadelphia would occur about 0230 the following morning. He could expect to dock at Philadelphia shortly before 0400 and the stevedores had been made aware of his arrival time, and that three 20-man gangs of longshoremen would be ready. The ship's agent was not particularly happy with having to load the *Rita E.* on a national holiday; the local Longshoreman's union expected triple-time payment for working the ship on July 4, but the home office agreed that remaining in compliance with the strict requirements of the contract was essential. After departing Baltimore the relief skipper would bring the *Rita E* south to transit through the Panama Canal, stopping at Pearl Harbor and Subic Bay in the Philippines for additional materials before delivering them to Cam Ranh Bay, RVN.

The services of a river pilot, licensed by the Pilots Association for the Bay and River Delaware, was essential. Even though the distance from the pilot station to Pier 4 South at the foot of Chestnut Street was only 86.5 nautical miles (~100 land miles) it was an extraordinarily busy waterway. At 14 knots average speed, it would take the *Rita E* at least 6 hours to arrive at Pier 4, and perhaps another 45 minutes, with the aid of tugs and a docking pilot, to tie up at the Pier. Although Tom held a USCG Unlimited Tonnage, (All Oceans) license as a Master Mariner, he had never approached the Port of Philadelphia before, and neither had his first mate, Joe Roy. Both would remain on the bridge, observing Anthony James, a pilot with more than 30 years experience on the river.

"Just call me A.J, everybody does," the affable pilot began. "Now, aside from outbound traffic, your major obstacles are going to be shoal water stretches, particularly on the New Jersey side of the river. The current now is only about 2 knots opposing us, but things get a little entertaining as we near the shoals. Once we're nearing the capes, the Hen and Chicken Shoal extends southeastward from the tip of Cape Henlopen. The shoal has depths of only 5 feet, 1.3 miles from the tip of the cape, so that's a real ship killer. And you've got to watch out for the The Cape May-Lewes Ferry crossing the main channel about 4 miles inside the bay, especially at night. Those ferry guys all have full pilot's licenses, but I wouldn't trust half of them to pilot a garbage scow."

He continued to provide running commentary throughout the dark and very foggy passage up to Philadelphia. "You've got Deadman's Shoal and Ship John Shoal to contend with, and don't forget the bridges, either. You've got the Delaware Memorial Bridge at mile 60, the Commodore Barry Bridge between Chester and Bridgeport at mile 71, and once you pass the Navy yard, you'll run under the Walt Whitman Bridge at mile 84. It's an stressful hundred miles up to Philly, I'm tellin' ya!"

Undaunted by the weather and the various obstacles described by the pilot, the *Rita E* continued her steady journey upriver. Just abreast of the Philadelphia Mercantile exchange on Walnut Street the pilot began a gentle turn aligning her with Pier 4 South. With her river pilot aboard and with generally favorable conditions she dismissed the tugs which were standing by and had lines on the pier shortly after 4:30 AM. An advance party of dockers was on hand to assist, and her starboard side was securely fastened to the downriver side of the pier within minutes. As her accommodation ladder was lowered, her ship's agent and the business agent of the Longshoreman's Association came board.

"Welcome to the Port of Philadelphia, skipper," the Longshoreman's business agent said with a handshake. "We have you set up for a quick turnaround. There are three full docker gangs at the shape-up point beneath the Benjamin Franklin Bridge, just about a quarter-mile north of here, and they will be down here on the pier within the next few minutes. Since it is so close to dawn, we'll skip setting up mobile floodlights, which will make the movement of cargo that much quicker. In the pier shed we've pre-positioned a fair amount of dry cargo for you, and along Delaware Avenue we've already moved about a dozen freight cars full of material from the government arsenals at Frankford (Philadelphia) and the Letterkenny Army Depot up at Chambersburg. There are several vehicles, including jeeps, 2 1/2 ton trucks and other specialized equipment, as well as about a half-million rounds of .227 ammunition for the new M-16s on flat cars which are being held for security reasons inside the Frankford Arsenal. These will be dispatched around 8:30 this morning. All in all, we expect to have you fully-loaded and ready to sail to to Locust Point in Baltimore, not much later than 4:00 PM."

"Your pilot is licensed to take you back down the river and through the Chesapeake and Delaware Canal, after which he'll swap out with a Chesapeake Bay pilot who will have you well into the Bay in time to make a safe landing at Baltimore shortly after dawn tomorrow."

Captain Tom and first mate Joe Roy reviewed the loading plan for the ship, which traditionally was submitted by the third mate. Concurrently, the docker gangs began arriving from the shape-up point and began their preparations to move the cargo aboard the *Rita E*. Shortly before 6 AM the first cargo nets swung over the side and loading began in earnest.

The shipping agent kept up a running commentary as the war materials came aboard. "You know, the longshoreman's unions in Philadelphia are unique among dockers around the country. From around 1900, Local Eight of The National Maritime Workers Union, an historically black dockers local, has been active here in Philly. The dockers of Local Eight worked side-by-side with the other, traditionally ethnically-based groups of dockworkers in the city."

"Doesn't that cause a lot of tension, especially in times like these?" asked Joe Roy, a fourth generation Cajun from the banks of Bayou Lafourche.

"Surprisingly, not as much as you might expect. We usually have multiple gangs, each working a particular section of the ship. Although gangs cooperate freely as needed, the gang bosses try to keep them separated while on board. The shape-ups are by union locals, of course, so things are fair in that respect."

Of the three gangs assigned to the *Rita E,* one was drawn exclusively from the black community. The other two gangs represented the Irish neighborhoods of Fishtown and Port Richmond, and the Italian neighborhoods of South Philadelphia which surrounded the city's docks. Most longshoremen were second and third generation dockworkers and guarded their privileges fiercely. *Hard work for hard men* was a sentiment heard frequently on the docks of Philadelphia and the union halls of the surrounding neighborhoods.

One fiercely-guarded privilege was the guaranteed lunch break granted regardless of the urgency of the cargo or the ship's schedule. Many of the dockers took their lunch break in one of several bars and cafés which lined the west side of Delaware Avenue, or frequented the small sandwich trucks, universally derided as "roach coaches" which parked along the pier head. Even their meal of choice, the grinder/poor boy locally known as the "hoagie," was named after the Hog Island shipyards, a few miles to the south. By 11:30 AM, many of the boxcars on the rails lining the center of Delaware Avenue were empty, and as the three gangs rotated through the lunch break, several dockers took the opportunity to sit in the open doorways of the boxcars to avoid the hot sun overhead.

S.S. Rita E. Sykes, a general (break bulk) freighter of Sykes Brothers Line

CHAPTER 4
HITTING ON THE DOCK OF THE BAY

Thursday, July 4, 1968 - Philadelphia

By the morning of July 4, 1968, fewer than 2000 demonstrators had gathered at the historic Quadrangle, the physical and spiritual center of the Penn campus. Protest leaders, including Joel Staghorn, waited well beyond the published 10 AM kick-off time in the hope that stragglers would soon appear, but by 10:30 the group was becoming restless and vocal. The SDS steward grabbed a bullhorn and harangued the crowd, causing several of the more rational students to abandon the protest in disgust.

"We're marching to Independence Hall! Let's show Philadelphia and the whole world what we think of this immoral war in Vietnam." Unfortunately, the collective decision to forgo a permit for the march also eliminated most of the publicity that they sought for their crusade. The local media outlets – TV Channels 3, 6, and 10, and local powerhouse KYW news-radio – relied on the Philadelphia police to inform of them of any such demonstrations. These notifications were usually based upon the permits issued. But, based on a tip from the Roundhouse, KYW-TV3, the NBC affiliate, did have a crew assembled on 18th street adjacent to Rittenhouse Square. Finally, nearly 45 minutes late, the march left the Quad and proceeded north through the tree-lined campus, before turning east on Walnut Street and crossing the Schuylkill River. As expected, the

University Police were nowhere to be seen, and the Philadelphia Police, under direct orders from City Hall, did nothing to interfere. The marchers arrived at Rittenhouse Square, picking up additional demonstrators to accompany the rag-tag procession, while banging drums and blowing whistles to the dismay of the well-heeled residents of the stately homes and luxury apartments surrounding the well-kept park.

The organizing committee had positioned the small PAVE contingent at the front line of the march, and had also invited Staghorn to address the group at the historic square, just to the west of Center City. Grasping the ubiquitous bullhorn, modern technology's gift to protesters everywhere, Staghorn addressed the singing, laughing and generally well-behaved marchers. "This is the 192nd anniversary of the Declaration of Independence. Vietnam has been independent for fewer than 20 years. We suffered under British rule for fewer than 200 years; the Vietnamese people have suffered first under the Chinese, and then the French, and now our own military for over 500 years. We look upon Thomas Payne, Paul Revere and all the signers of the Declaration of Independence as our national heroes. Who do you think the Vietnamese look upon as their heroes? It's not General Abrams or General Westmoreland, that's for sure. It's General Giap and Ho Che Minh that they look to for deliverance from their oppressors. And who are their oppressors? Not just the government of the United States, but rather each and every one of us who fails to stop this criminal conspiracy of the military industrial complex which oppresses not only the Vietnamese people but all of the freedom-loving peoples of the world. We're going to continue to Independence Hall, where our vaunted independence was declared, and declare for the Vietnamese people independence from LBJ, and from Dow Chemical, and Boeing, and from all of our criminal war gangs. Let the peaceful march of a peaceful people continue!"

Unobserved by Staghorn or any of his key lieutenants, small groups of other protesters had begun to infiltrate the march while passing through

Rittenhouse Square. As the original marchers exited the square, even more outsiders joined the fringes of the protest, and when the group was detoured north to Chestnut Street by police barricades placed by the traffic division, these infiltrators, many of whom were affiliated with the Panthers or anarchist groups, took up tactical positions at the center of the protest march. Others had infiltrated the group as well, including undercover police officers from both the civil disobedience squad and the stakeout unit. They took up positions on the flanks of the main march and continued in those critical positions as the group made its way, noisily but essentially peacefully, down Chestnut Street through the city's premier shopping distinct toward Independence National Historical Park, a 55-acre oasis of stately buildings centered upon Independence Hall.

As noon approached, the police presence became much more visible along the route, particularly as the marchers continued east on Chestnut. Larger numbers of police, including the full civil disobedience squad and the motorcycle-mounted officers of the city's famed Highway Patrol (which, despite its nondescript name, was really the elite, city-wide tactic response team) were also lined up along the side streets leading to the historic icon. When they reached the park, the protesters were met by a solid phalanx of the National Park Police, many of whom had been brought in from other sites throughout the state. Belying their gentle "Ranger Rick" image, these helmeted federal officers, equipped with modern firearms, ballistic vests, shields and riot sticks, were aligned in such a way to deny entry by protesters and to protect the hall and the famed Liberty Bell at all costs.

Staghorn went forward to meet with the National Park Police, and to explain that this was a peaceful protest, and that they should expect no trouble from the pacifists. But before he could speak, a hail of bricks, M-60 firecrackers and urine-filled balloons launched by the interlopers began to rain down upon the front of the crowd. Chanting "One, two, three, four – We don't want your Fucking War," and other obscenities, as the intruders became more vocal and less controlled by the stewards, Philadelphia police units entered the area from all directions. Most of the anarchists and other militants moved back onto Chestnut Street, and with the Philadelphia police in hot pursuit, ran east toward the Delaware river. As they crossed Delaware Avenue, the spotted a large stockpile of military supplies being loaded on a freighter docked at Pier 4 South at the foot of Chestnut Street. Chanting "LBJ, LBJ, how many kids did you kill today?" and "Ho Ho Ho, Ho Chi Minh," they sprinted around a number of boxcars halted on the railroad tracks in the middle of Delaware Avenue and approached the sheds which lined the pier.

As they worked the *Rita E,* the dockers could hear the disturbance further up Chestnut Street. As they rushed to watch, they spotted large groups of demonstrators running east on Chestnut Street toward them, with the police firing tear gas in hot pursuit. Many dockers quickly availed themselves of short pieces of pipe or nail-studded boards, and most were carrying cargo hooks in the belt loops of their dungarees. [Before the age of containerization, freight was handled by extensive manual labor, and the longshoreman's hook was the basic tool of the dockworker. It even became the informal symbol of the trade. When longshoremen in Philadelphia went on strike or retired, it became known as "hanging up the hook" or "slinging the hook," and the newsletter for retired members of the International Longshoremen and Warehousemen's Union was named *The Rusty Hook.*]

Spotting the dockers blocking the east end of Chestnut Street, the protesters realized that they were trapped between serious injury and the Delaware River. Several in the front began pleading with the dock workers to allow them through. But when it became clear that this was an antiwar protest, and that the *Rita E* was loading materials for shipment to Vietnam, the tenor of the conversations changed. Most of the dockers were military veterans, either of the Second World War, or the Korean conflict. Others had sons or other close relatives who had fought in or were fighting in Vietnam. As the first rocks and paving stones struck the wall of longshoremen, retaliation was immediate. Big Bill Jackson, 6' 6" and 255 pounds, the ganger of Local Eight's crew shouted, "Don't let them get on the pier, and whatever you do, don't let them get near the ship!" It quickly became a pitched battle, and the most serious antiwar rioting that had occurred to date. Nevertheless, dozens of protesters/rioters made an end run around the parked railroad train, and poured through the open gates leading to Pier 4S. As they swarmed the pier, chased by longshoremen and with the Philadelphia Police Department in hot pursuit, the protesters were intercepted by the other loading gangs and indiscriminate and brutal carnage was the predictable result.

Protest marchers en-route to Independence Hall on July 4, 1968

S.S. Rita E, Sykes loading cargo destined for Vietnam shortly before the riot

CHAPTER 5
THE GOOD SAMARITAN

Thursday, July 4, 1968 - Delaware River

One young woman, bleeding extensively but still more fortunate than many others, in desperation sought refuge aboard the *Rita E*. While the crew was distracted by the commotion, she managed to crawl up the accommodation ladder. Severely battered and bleeding profusely from a 9-inch cut on her forehead caused by a wildly swung cargo hook, she was hardly able to crawl across the deck before collapsing behind a pile of large wooden crates. Drifting in and out of consciousness, she remained in hiding while the Philadelphia police regained control of the pier, arresting any protesters found in the restricted area of the port.

The Battle of the Docks, as it later became known, lasted for fewer than fifteen minutes, although to the participants it certainly felt as if it had lasted for hours. The demonstrators scattered both north and south on Delaware Avenue, and the police roughly interrogated everyone whom they believed either participated in or witnessed the scuffle. Not surprisingly, most of the dockers claimed to have been deep in the hold of the *Rita E* at the time, and the police themselves left within an hour. The total impact upon the loading of the vessel was minimal; it had been, when all was said and done, just an extended lunch break for the dockers involved.

By 3:30 PM, the cargo had been loaded and stowed, and by 4:00 PM the river pilot had returned to the ship. "High tide is expected at 4:48 PM today. If we can get all the lines in, we can make the tide and be headed down river toward the Chesapeake and Delaware Canal. It's about 48 nautical miles downstream from here, and we should be abeam Reedy Point by about 6:00 PM or so. The canal is only 14 miles long, and at this time of year you should just be about through the canal by dusk."

"Let's get underway then," said Captain Tom, "I've had enough of Philadelphia for one trip!"

They were midstream in the Delaware River at about 4:15 that afternoon. As they made their way downstream, Jess Orwin, the ship's boatswain, made his usual sweep of the main deck cleaning up any potential flotsam before entering the narrow canal at Reedy Point. While securing a number of small containers, he discovered the young woman, still bleeding profusely from the cut on her forehead, and still in a state of semiconsciousness. "Skipper, you want to get down here real quick like!" he shouted. "I don't know if you want to call this a stowaway or what, but we've got a visitor on board!"

Captain Carpentier raced to the weather decks and helped Orwin gently move the young woman away from the crates of cargo where she had taken refuge. "Jess, get a couple of your guys from the deck gang to help this young lady up to my cabin. Send somebody for the medical supply box as well. She's taken a nasty whack on the head, and it looks like she somehow sought refuge up here during the melee in fear for her life. Turning to the young woman, he reassured her: "Don't be frightened, young lady, you're in good hands now and far enough downstream that no one can hurt you."

She was quickly removed to the captain's stateroom, and Jess, a former army medic who worked as a paramedic while ashore, soon treated the cut on the left side of her forehead and the bumps and bruises on her scalp. "She doesn't look real bad, Skipper, but I bet it knocked her for a loop there for a couple of minutes. I don't think that we should attempt stitches, but she ought to see a doctor when she gets a chance. Maybe bandages, and some more rest to get over the excitement of the afternoon, is the best thing we can give her right now."

"I think you're right. We can't turn around in the river, but she can lie here and rest in my cabin until we get down to Baltimore and we can have our ship's agent drive her, either to a hospital there or, if she feels up to it, to the Trailways bus station to catch a ride home."

"Can you tell me your name, young lady?"

"My name is Becky. Becky Franks. I'm so embarrassed that I've inconvenienced you but when all of those big men swinging hooks attacked us, I'm afraid I just panicked. I didn't know where I was going, but I knew I needed to get out of there as quickly as I could."

"What were you doing there anyway? When the police came aboard they said that that was not an authorized protest. How did you get involved in all of that?"

"Well, I'm a nursing student at University Hospital. I've actually been an RN for several years, but I decided I wanted to finish my BSN degree, and started at the University of Pennsylvania Hospital last September. Some of the other nurses and doctors were going along for the march against the Vietnam war, and I just decided to tag along to see what it was all about. I really do hate it that all these young guys are getting killed in Vietnam. Some of my friends work at the Naval Hospital in South Philly, and they tell me how horrific many of the injuries are. I had no idea what I was getting myself into."

Tom replied, "Well, if it's any consolation, I don't think any of us anticipated what happened earlier today. The police officer who took my statement said that it was a generally peaceful demonstration, until some radicals infiltrated the crowd and began throwing rocks. And we were just down here loading materials and trying to get out of Philadelphia in time to get to Baltimore early tomorrow morning. Ironically, we are under charter to the Military Sea Transportation Service and the ship will eventually make its way across the Pacific to Vietnam itself."

"You mean you're going all the way across to Vietnam in this ship? How long will that take you?"

"Actually, I'm not going but the ship is. I brought her across from Belgium, and stopped in New York and Philadelphia, and we're now heading down to Locust Point in Baltimore, where I'll turn the old *Rita E* over to my relief. He'll run her down and through the Panama Canal and across the Pacific arriving in Vietnam, oh, sometime in September, I would think. Then he'll bring her back and I'll pick her up in Baltimore and have her for the next six months or so after that."

"Wow! Nice work if you can get it, I guess. I'm from up in the coal regions of central Pennsylvania and I've never met anyone who is a mariner, although my dad was in the Navy right before World War II."

"I was in World War II myself. I started out at the Maine Maritime Academy before the war, and wound up spending all my Navy career in the North Atlantic. Where was your dad stationed?"

"I don't really know much about my dad; he died when I was little. His ship was sunk by the Germans even before the war started. It was called the *Reuben James*, but all I know about it is the little bit my mother told me, and that song by Woody Guthrie. I wish I knew more about my father and what happened to him."

"I know a little bit about the *Reuben James*. In 1941, I was stationed at a place called Argentia, Newfoundland. The *Reuben James* was part of a destroyer squadron that escorted convoys between Canada and Iceland and often came into the base at Argentia. I don't recall ever speaking to anyone on your dad's ship, but you're right; she was sunk just before the Japanese attacked us at Pearl Harbor, and we entered the war against both the Japanese and the Germans a short time later. I'm sorry for your loss; I'm sure your dad was a very brave man. Anyone who served in the North Atlantic had a very tough job. Even in peacetime, the North Atlantic is not anywhere you would want to be, particularly in the late autumn or early winter. He was a brave man, Miss Franks."

"Please, call me Becky or even Frankie. That's the nickname other nurses gave me when I was in nursing school. And yes, I suppose he was a brave man, I only wish I knew him better. May I tell you something?"

Captain Tom nodded.

"The last time I saw my father I was just four years old. I remember that I was acting terribly. I don't know if I sensed somehow that he was going away again, or that I was overly tired, or if I had a cold, or I was just being a bratty four-year old. We had gone out for dinner to a restaurant in Tremont, and I really acted horribly. When we got home, I was defiant to my mother, and my dad in desperation took off his belt and gave me a couple really good whacks across my backside. He told me to go to my room, and as I stomped up the stairs I shouted 'I hate you, I hate you!' and slammed the door of my room. Those were the last words I ever spoke to my father..."

She sat there for a long moment with tears in her eyes.

Tom Carpentier also sat quietly. He really did not know what to say, but sensed intuitively that saying nothing was better than uttering polite, meaningless words. After a few moments, he could feel the slow turn to starboard which indicated that the ship had reached the entrance to the Chesapeake and Delaware canal.

"I have an idea," he said to his unexpected passenger. "I have to head back up to the bridge. It will take us about an hour to let the up-bound vessels clear the canal. If you are feeling up to it then, why not go out on one of the bridge wings, and you'll experience a view unlike one you'll find anywhere. The canal is only 450 feet wide, and the *Rita E's* beam is nearly 65 feet. With the curvature of the hull, from the bridge it feels like the ship is sailing through open fields on either side. It's a real delight."

The bleeding from her head injury had abated somewhat, thanks to the ministrations of Boatswain Orwin, and Becky readily agreed. As promised the view was unsurpassed. Within an hour the vessel had reached Chesapeake City, and the pilot boat came alongside to exchange the Delaware River pilot for one qualified on the waters of Chesapeake Bay.

When the pilot exchange had been completed safely, Captain Tom came out on the port side bridge wing and joined the young nurse. "I have an idea, Becky" he began. "It'll take me a couple of hours, once we arrive at Locust Point, to brief my relief, sign the necessary paperwork and turn the ship over to him. I have a condominium out in Catonsville. After you've been treated, why don't you visit with me for a day or two and we can explore the National Archives and the Navy Historical Center in Washington to see what we can learn about your dad and the last days of the *Reuben James*. I live alone, and while the condo is nothing special, it will give you a chance to recover a bit, and maybe answer a few questions that have gone unanswered for the last 28 years or so. I have a car available to me, and I can get you around town if you like."

"That is terribly kind of you Captain, but I can't impose upon you that way."

"It's no imposition at all, Becky. Truth be told, the hardest part of being ashore for me is finding something interesting to do. I often go down to Washington, to the various museums on the mall or to spend the day at the Library of Congress. I certainly welcome the company."

"Do you think we'll learn anything more about the *Reuben James* that we don't know already?"

"We won't know until we look, will we? I do know that the Navy Historical Center at the Washington Navy Yard is a treasure trove of original materials, some of it dating back to the Revolutionary War days. Even if you can't come along, you've whet my appetite and I'll probably go over there sometime within a few days to see what I can find."

"Well, my last semester ended on June 30, and I have no classes scheduled until after Labor Day. I was planning on heading up to Schuylkill County to visit my family, but they're not expecting me until later this month. I'll have the doctors check out these knots on my head. They'll no doubt want to add a few sutures too. I'll pick up some clothes, farm out my cats, and we'll go."

CHAPTER 6
OF FATHERS AND DAUGHTERS

Friday, July 19, 1968 - Baltimore

Captain Tom and Becky had exchanged telephone numbers before she left to return to Philadelphia. Because of her visible injuries, the Sykes Brothers shipping agent had agreed to drive her directly back to the Quaker City, and she arrived there shortly before 2 PM on Friday. She was treated by her colleagues at University Hospital, and after two weeks dedicated to rest and recovery, was feeling noticeably better. Taking Tom up on his invitation, she phoned him and arranged to meet him at the Trailways bus depot in downtown Baltimore.

Captain Tom was pleased to see her again. He drove her to suburban Catonsville where the Sykes Brothers Line maintained a condominium for its captains who were temporarily ashore. Plainly furnished, and located just off busy Frederick Road, it was nevertheless convenient to both the city of Baltimore and the thriving areas of Baltimore County.

Tom opened the door for her. "It's not very big, and it's not the way that I would decorate it, but it's free and it's worth every dime I pay for it. There are two full bedrooms, and a nice patio which gets a good breeze even in midsummer. You're welcome to stay in the guest room as long as I am ashore. I should be here until mid-November, unless we have a situation where another captain needs early relief. Make yourself at home."

Becky looked around. It was indeed sparsely furnished but there were several photographs on shelves in the living room. The largest photograph showed a middle-aged woman standing with a younger woman, no doubt her daughter, at a college graduation ceremony. There were other photographs of the younger woman in a military uniform.

As she looked carefully at the photographs, Captain Tom commented. "That's my wife and my daughter. The photographs were taken when my daughter graduated from the University of Maine in Orono a few years back. Unfortunately, I was off the coast of East Africa at the time and could not get home."

"Your daughter looks a lot like you," Becky commented. "She's about as tall as you are and has your eyes. But tell me, where is your wife now?" she questioned.

"It's a long story," Tom replied. "I met my wife in Newfoundland, in the latter part of 1940. We married in the fall of 1941, with war fast approaching. When I resigned my Navy commission in 1946, well, the only skill I had was the ability to drive ships through the ocean. Even my college education was directed that way; I earned my bachelors degree in Marine engineering back in 1936."

"I was fortunate to get a good job with Sykes Brothers, and my wife, my daughter and I moved to Algiers, Louisiana right across the river from New Orleans. I shipped out as third mate on Sykes Brother's freighters traveling around the world. I got home as often as I could, but my wife as a native Newfoundlander found the heat and humidity of Louisiana stifling. She also missed her family terribly. In those days even long distance service to the Canadian Maritimes was spotty, and terribly expensive. Finally, when I had just returned from a long trip around South America, she told me that our marriage was not working and that she was leaving me and taking our daughter, Mary Kay, with her. The news was devastating, but not totally unexpected. I still love her, and she still loves me, but having an absentee husband and an absentee father was not what she envisioned when we married. I bought her tickets back to St. John's and that's where she lives today. We're still married – both of us are Roman Catholic – so divorce is not really an option. But she has her life as a teacher, and I have mine. I do get up there for a month or so every time I'm ashore."

"And what about your daughter? Where is she now?

Captain Tom sat quietly for a long moment, staring out into busy Fredrick Road. "Because she had dual citizenship she was able to enroll in the nursing program at the University of Maine. She received, essentially, a free-ride scholarship sponsored by the Navy Nurse Corps and she graduated from that program in 1964. I was very proud of her, and even more proud that she chose to follow me into the Navy. I was able to visit with her a number of times when she was stationed at the Naval Hospital on Staten Island. But two years ago she received orders to Vietnam. She was assigned first to the hospital ship *USS Sanctuary* off the coast of the DMZ, and then temporarily to the Naval Support Activity at Danang. She was killed there 18 months ago."

There was complete silence in the room. Neither spoke. Finally, Becky said; "Oh Tom, that's horrible. I'm so terribly sorry for your loss. What happened?"

Tom Carpentier sat silently, looking off into the distance. "Yes, I was devastated when I received the telegram from the Navy Department. Once again, I was off at sea. Did you know the Navy has a program for its submarine sailors concerning things like this? Before they depart on a patrol, they check off a form which says something like 'if something bad happens I want to know' or 'if something bad happens, don't tell me while I'm at sea.' I wish there were something similar for those of us in the Merchant Marine. I was in mid-Pacific, heading back to the states from Japan and there was nothing I could do. I managed to get a radio-telephone call back to my wife, who was even more distraught than I. Then once I got back to Tacoma, Sykes Brothers had a relief skipper waiting on the dock. He wouldn't even let me do the turnover paperwork. He just said 'Go.' He handed me airline tickets, first from Seattle to Vancouver BC, and then a first-class ticket on Air Canada all the way to St. John's, Newfoundland. I met my wife and members of her family, and we mourned together."

"The Navy took care of all the logistics from their side, and a few weeks later we met her body at Dover Air Force Base in Delaware. She had signed some paperwork saying that, if anything happened, she would like to have her body cremated, and we honored her final wishes. Her ashes were finally buried in Newfoundland, in her mother's family plot."

"I don't mean to pry, but how did it happen? Was it an enemy attack on the hospital there at Danang?"

"That's where things begin to take some strange turns. The Navy said yes, it was 'combat related,' whatever the hell that means. I checked, and there were no reported incidents of attack, nor sniper fire, nor any other enemy action at the base between the date of her death and the date her body was shipped to Dover. Nothing whatsoever. I checked with the other military services too, they have no record. I even checked with the United Press International and Associated Press offices in New York. Their correspondents have no record of any hostile action during those days, either in Danang or anywhere else in Quang Nam province which surrounds the naval base. So what happened? When we received her body back it was in a sealed metal coffin and we were not permitted to open it or see her body. The cremation took place just a short time later."

"Tom, that's a terrible story. How could the military be so callous and crass? I thought that the Navy and Marine Corps took care of of their own."

"Well, that's what I thought when I was on active duty during World War II. Maybe things have changed, I don't know. But this I do know – I will not rest until I find out what happened to my little girl. When you told me the story of your father, well, I don't know what it was that brought you on the *Rita E* on the docks in Philadelphia, be it fate or karma or just coincidence. But whatever it was, you and I both share empty spots in our hearts, and I for one will do everything to get those holes filled. And we can start tomorrow in Washington."

Becky, still feeling the effects of her recent injuries decided to rest for the afternoon. She awoke shortly after 5 PM, freshened up, and admitted to being ravishingly hungry.

"Would you like to go somewhere really special for dinner?" Tom asked. "Baltimore of course is famous for its seafood, particularly for blue crabs, and there's a restaurant not far from here which is particularly good."

"I've never had blue crabs before," Becky replied. "Are they actually blue?"

"Well, not after they been steamed," Tom explained. "But they do have a greenish-blue appearance when they've first been caught. You can find them all up and down the East Coast, but the ones caught in the waters of Chesapeake Bay are really special. After they've been boiled, they turn red."

"Sounds great to me! As long as we don't have to go down to the port to get them. Being attacked by those dockworkers has turned me off on walking around piers and wharves for a while."

"No worries there, Becky. The place I have in mind is just about a mile or so down Frederick Road and just inside the Baltimore city limits. I think that's one reason why Sykes Brothers chose Catonsville as the rest area for captains ashore in Baltimore. Unfortunately, docks and shipyards are rarely found in the nicer parts of town. I understand that Baltimore intends to to clean up the so-called Inner Harbor area, down along E. Baltimore Street. Personally, I'll believe that when I see it, but being out here in the Western suburbs gives us mariners a chance to live like normal people for a while. There's an old saying among sailors: When I retire I'm going to take a long oar over my shoulder and start walking. When somebody asks me 'What's that thing?' – That's where I'm going to settle."

"From what I can see, neither Philadelphia nor Baltimore will suit you then!"

Tom was right. It was just a 10-minute drive to Kavanaugh's Famous Sea Food on Frederick Avenue just inside the city. With over 100 years in the business, its stellar reputation for quality was both local and regional. Tom had made reservations, and it was a very short wait until they were shown to their table. As they were walking toward the rear of the restaurant, Tom spotted two familiar faces at an aisle table. After placing their orders, Tom asked. "Do you see those two fellows over there by the window? Do you know who they are?"

Becky turned briefly and looked. "You mean the two middle-aged guys, one with the beard and the other clean shaven?"

"Yes, those two guys. They're rather famous these days."

Becky shook her head no.

"Those are the Kerrigan Brothers, Dan and Philip. Both of them are Catholic priests. One of them, in fact, is at St. Martin of Tours parish here in West Baltimore. The other is a Jesuit; I believe he lives in New York. Back in May they led a protest at the selective service offices in Catonsville. Ironically, the office was in the old Knights of Columbus hall, just down the road from my condo. They confiscated over 300 draft records, took them to the parking lot and burned them. Unlike the radicals and anarchists who had hijacked your protest march in Philadelphia, the Kerrigan Brothers and their seven associates waited patiently for the police to come and arrest them. Personally, I much prefer their style of protest of the Vietnam War to the way things deteriorated in Philadelphia."

"Well, in retrospect, so do I," commented Becky. "Up in Schuylkill County where I am from, almost every guy between the ages of 18 and 25 has either been drafted or expects to be drafted, and 90% of them wind up in the infantry, and most of those in Vietnam. When I was a little girl, I always wished for a brother. Now I'm glad my wish never came true. They're just recruiting cannon fodder, as far as I can tell."

"Yeah, I always wished for a son. But if I had one now, I would buy him a one-way ticket back to Newfoundland. I don't always agree with the Canadians, but this time I think they got it right."

Their dinners arrived, and both agreed that the Chesapeake blue crabs lived up to their expectations. After coffee and dessert, they left Kavanaugh's and on the way out passed the Kerrigans. Tom nodded and thought to himself, "God bless you both."

"Let's call it a night, Tom. If were going to head down to Washington tomorrow, it's best that we get an early start."

"You're right, Becky. I don't know if you've ever driven the Baltimore-Washington Parkway but rush-hour can be a very trying experience, particularly down between Fort Meade and the cut-off heading toward Annapolis. We'll want a good night's sleep. I've arranged a meeting with the director of the Navy Historical Center at the Navy Yard in Southeast Washington for 10 AM, and we'll will want to be well rested."

"Do you think either one of us will find what we're looking for?"

"As I said earlier, we won't know until we look, will we?"

Awakening early the next morning, and after stopping for coffee at the local Dunkin' Donuts, Tom and Becky headed south on the Baltimore-Washington Parkway toward the Washington Navy Yard. It housed among other things, the Chief of Naval Operations office and the Navy Historical Center. The hour and a half drive through morning commuter traffic gave Tom and Becky some 'windshield time' to chat with each other.

"Tell me more about yourself, if you like," Tom said. Have you always lived in Pennsylvania?"

"Yes, I have. My family all live in the coal-regions, about 100 miles northwest of Philadelphia. My grandfather was a miner, and later man-ager of a large mine owned by the Reading Coal Company. He died of black-lung disease long before I was born. My grandmother still lives in a wooden duplex, part of a former coal-camp on the side of a mountain halfway between Pine Grove and Tremont. I went to high school there in Porter Township; our school was so small that my graduating class consisted of eight girls and four boys. I played basketball there, even though I'm not very tall. But I was darn good basketball player! I was fortunate to be able to attend a three-year nursing program in Reading, about 50 miles east of where I grew up. I moved to Philadelphia, and, well, you know the rest."

"I suppose you had a lots of boyfriends, eh?"

"Not as many as you might suspect, nor as many as I would like!" she replied, laughing. Although I'm dating a Dutch doctor these days; between the workload of nursing school, and then trying to make a living as an RN while I sent every dime I could back to support my mom, there hasn't been a lot of extra time left for dating. And most of the guys that I have dated, well, they're not the type you would take home to your mother, if you know what I mean."

Tom laughed. "May I tell you something?" he asked.

"You can. You know, I feel very comfortable with you. You're about what I expect my dad to be like, had he lived."

"You remind me a great deal of my daughter, too. I don't know if that's because both of you attended nursing school, and pretty much made your own way in the world, or what. But I suspect if she were still here she would like you a lot, and you would like her. She wasn't a basketball player; her sports were softball and soccer. She actually tried out for the soccer team when she was at the University of Maine, but she ran into the same problem you had. There just weren't enough hours in the day, nor days in the week for her to do everything she would have liked to do. In one of the last letters I got from her after she had arrived in Danang, she talked about watching the little kids at a local orphanage kicking around a beat-up old soccer ball that someone had donated to them. She loved little kids, and had planned on helping out at the orphanage, but then..."

"You remind me of my father too, Tom. Not that I remember all that much about him, but my mom talked about him a lot when I was growing up. It was just me and her then, and she was always working it seemed, first as a telephone operator and then when she and her sister bought an old, beat-up taproom on the only state route out of town. They worked their butts off to make it successful, and I guess that they did. But running a bar takes a lot of effort, and I wish I had had more time with her when I was growing up. The one good thing is that it made me independent at a very young age, and I suppose that has served me well as I grew older. But if she had been in Philadelphia last week she would have cautioned me in no uncertain terms to stay as far away from the demonstration as possible. I don't know that I would have taken her advice, but now I wish that that I had stayed away!"

CHAPTER 7
SHIPMATES REUNITED

Monday, July 22, 1968 – Washington

They finally arrived at the front gate of the Washington Navy Yard. After explaining the purpose of their visit to the Marine sentry, he gave them directions to the Historical Center and waved them through. It just took a few seconds more to arrive at their destination.

Tom looked at his watch. "We made it down from Baltimore in pretty good time," he said. "We have about 10 minutes before our appointment with the director. Do you want to go in and freshen up before we see him?"

"I sure do. Remind me not to get an extra large coffee again if we are going to make a long trip!"

After a short personal break for each of them, they met again in the director's outer office. His secretary greeted them and in a moments time ushered them in. VADM Harry "Tincan" Tomsen (ret.) rose and greeted them with a wide smile. "I thought I recognized that name when you called for an appointment, Tom. Or should I still call you 'sir'?"

"Harry Tomsen! My God, sir, it's been almost 25 years! This *is* a surprise. When last I saw you, you were just a dumb-ass ensign, and I was your skipper on the *USS Dennis N. Terry!* You were a regular dufus back then, and now it says on your door that you're a retired vice admiral? I knew I should have stayed in after 1946!"

"That was me, Tom, and I was as drifty an ensign as ever made it through Ohio State's RTOC program. If you hadn't taken me under your wing in those first days, I might have just said the hell with it, and jumped over the side. But, hey, you're not doing that badly yourself, Tom. I understand you're the master of a merchant vessel these days. You can be sure of one thing, the money in your line of work is a heck of a lot better than Navy pay, I can tell you. But who is this lovely young lady you've brought to see me?"

Tom introduced Becky Franks to the director. He briefly explained how they came to meet each other. "Becky has a special interest in what happened to the *Reuben James* back in October 1941. She lost her dad on that ship."

"I'm sorry to hear that, Miss Franks. I don't know how much we will be able to help you to understand what happened that day, but I have asked Dr. Anne K. Dellinger to offer you whatever assistance we can. Annie is our curator for all the materials relating to Navy activity in the Atlantic theater. She's quite knowledgeable; she came to the Naval Historical Center from the staff of Dr. Samuel Eliot Morison at Harvard University. Sam, as you may remember, wrote the definitive *History of the Navy in World War II,* and retired as a rear admiral in the Navy Reserve. Annie knows where all the bodies are buried; in fact, I think she acted as a gravedigger for Sam on more than one occasion. I'll tell you, Tom, one of the things I learned from moving from the fleet to academia is that history is whatever the historians want it to be."

He opened his door and asked his secretary to summon Dr. Dellinger, who arrived within a few moments and greeted her visitors with a smile. "Admiral Tomsen told me you were coming and told me a little bit about your interests. I will be glad to help however I can and I'm sure we'll find enough information to answer your questions."

"Annie, why don't you and Miss Franks go and explore the archives for a while. I'll sit here and chat about old times with Captain Carpentier for a few minutes before my next appointment."

After the women had left the office, the admiral came around his desk and sat face-to-face with Tom. "I'm terribly sorry about your loss, Tom. It must have come as a horrible shock to you. Both of my boys are flying combat missions in Vietnam right now, and their mother and I are terrified of seeing a chaplain coming up the front steps of our house. But your only daughter--I cannot even begin to comprehend the sense of loss you must feel."

"Thanks, Tincan, and I hope you and your wife never have to go through this. It threw me for a loop, it really did. And the worst part is, no one wants to own up to whatever happened. I've been stonewalled from day one, and being at sea most of the time didn't make it any easier. I seriously considered jumping ship at *Cam Ranh Bay* during my last trip over and heading up to I Corps to see for myself, but my first mate talked me out of it. He rightly reminded me that without orders or some documentation, I'd likely be shot before I made it off the base."

"Well, I've taken the liberty of nosing around Washington since I got your phone message. I've set up an appointment for you at 1 PM this afternoon with Captain Beatrice Conroy, the Chief of the Navy Nurse Corps. She's over at Arlington Hall, the Navy Annex. She's a tough old bird from what I've been told; she used to carry Florence Nightingale's spare lamps back in the Crimea, I think. I don't have any idea what she might know, or how much help she can be, but you and I can take a ride over there while Annie and Becky are working through the World War II files. One of the few perks of being a desk jockey these days is that the Navy still allows me to have a staff car and driver. I'll be happy to go along with you."

*　*　*

After leaving their two male colleagues behind, Becky Franks and Dr. Dellinger proceeded down the corridor and up a single flight of steps to Dr. Dellinger's office. "By the way," said Dr. Dellinger. "Please call me Annie. Everyone else does!"

When they reached her office, Dr. Dellinger unlocked the door. Compared to the director's office it was tiny, and while his office reflected the sense of organization which a career in the military fostered, Dr. Dellinger's office reflected her life in academia. There were books, boxes, and piles of papers everywhere. Even the guest chair was piled high with manuscripts. "Well, as the old song goes, 'If We Knew You Were Coming, We'd Have Baked a Cake.' I don't usually get many visitors, and when I do, I usually hijack a conference room somewhere in the building. But the good news about meeting up here is that, well, what you see is pretty much what you'll get."

Becky laughed. "It looks like you've been here for, well, several hundred years maybe?"

"Well, I'm a historian, aren't I? And I tell you, if it's not in this room, it probably doesn't exist. I may even have George Washington's wooden teeth somewhere around here. I think I saw them just a week or so ago."

Becky laughed again. She intuitively felt a connection with this gray-haired, short and slender woman. In some ways Dr. Annie reminded her of her mom. "How long have you been with the Naval Historical Center?"

"Not nearly as long as this mess might have you believe! I actually spent most of my life teaching. I earned my undergraduate degree at Smith, and my graduate degrees from Boston College. I taught at Boston College for a few years, and when President Roosevelt asked Dr. Morrison to write the definitive history of the Navy's contribution to World War II, he asked me to join him in what I thought would be a relatively simple project. I suggested that *Haze Gray and Underway* would be a good title for what I thought would probably be a 300-page volume with pictures. Fifteen volumes, and God only knows how many pages later, we delivered the final product to the Department of the Navy. Somewhere in all of this clutter are a number of sources for material that went into the books. You're looking at a life's work here, Becky!"

"Wow! That is fantastic Dr. Annie. May I call you that? It seems just a little more appropriate than just calling you Annie. You're about the same age as my mother, I'd say, and if I dared call her or any of her friends by their first names, she'd have knocked me into tomorrow."

"Why is it that everyone wants to make me old? I think I'm going to go home and dye my hair blonde. I'd have sailors hanging off me when I came to work the next day. But enough about me. Tell me a little bit about your dad. Let's start with his name. And do you happen to know anything about his service? Was he an officer or enlisted? And if he were enlisted, what was his rate and rating, do you know?"

"Well his name was George T. Franks, and I think he enlisted at Pottsville, Pennsylvania. He'd been in for several years and I believe his rating was machinist mate, 2nd class. My mom told me that he wasn't supposed to be on the *Reuben James*, but at the last minute another sailor became ill with appendicitis, and he received orders to go on patrol on the *James*. I guess that's when fate, or karma, or destiny, or whatever the heck you call it, kicked in. Had things gone differently he probably would have gotten off the *Reuben James* in Iceland and sailed back on another ship."

Dr. Annie rummaged through a pile of papers that had been set aside on her desk. "When the admiral told me you were coming, I dug around in some of the source data for the Morrison series, and pulled out a few things which we might find helpful. Ah, here's something we might use. It's the crew list as of the date of sailing from the the base at Argentia. I let me look – ah, sure enough, here he is listed among the petty officers on board." She handed the crew list to Becky.

"That makes me feel both happy and sad at the same time," Becky replied. I knew he was on the ship, at least that's what the telegram that my mother received had said."

"Yes, in general the Navy is pretty darn good at getting that right, at least." Here are some other things that I found regarding the *Reuben James*."

She handed three documents to Becky.

The first was a short biography of the ships namesake:

Reuben James of Delaware was a Navy boatswain's mate, famous for his heroism in the First Barbary War. Born in Delaware around 1776; when the *USS Philadelphia* was captured by the Barbary pirates when it ran aground in Tripoli, Lieutenant Stephan Decatur became locked in hand-to-hand combat while another enemy sailor swung his saber at him. Reuben James interposed himself between the descending sword and his commander, taking the blow on his head. The blow was not fatal and he continued his Naval career, serving many years with Decatur. He was forced to retire in January 1836 because of ill health. He died in 1838 at the U.S. Naval Hospital in Washington, DC.

"The site of the old hospital is just around the corner, by the way." she said. "The next contains an abbreviated summary of the ship's history since commissioning:"

USS Reuben James, (DD-245) was a post-World War I, four-funnel Clemson-class destroyer. Laid down on 2 April 1919 by the New York Shipbuilding Corporation in Camden, New Jersey and launched on 4 October 1919, she was commissioned 24 September 1920, too late for service in WW-I.

USS Reuben James saw extensive peacetime service in both the Atlantic and the Mediterranean until the outbreak of WW-II. In September 1939, *USS Reuben James* joined the Neutrality Patrol, first guarding critical Caribbean approaches to the American coast. In March, 1941, *Reuben James* joined the convoy escort force established to promote the safe arrival of materiel to the United Kingdom. This escort force guarded convoys as far as Iceland, after which they became the responsibility of British escorts.

Temporarily based in Iceland, *USS Reuben James* sailed from Naval Station Argentina, Newfoundland, on 23 October 1941, with four other destroyers to escort eastbound convoy HX 156. At about 0525 on 31 October, while escorting that convoy, *Reuben James* was torpedoed near Iceland. *Reuben James* had positioned herself between an ammunition ship in the convoy and the known position of a "wolf pack" *Reuben James* was hit forward by a torpedo meant for a merchant ship and her entire bow was blown off when a magazine exploded. The bow sank immediately, while the aft section floated for five minutes before going down. Of the 159-man crew, only 44 survived. The *USS Reuben James* was the first US warship to be deliberately sunk by Germany in WWII.

The third document was most interesting. Attached was an 11 X 13 black and white photograph of the ship, taken no doubt during her pre-commissioning trials, and all of her basic specifications.

Name: USS Reuben James DD-245

Builder: New York Shipbuilding **Laid down**: 2 April 1919 **Launched**: 4 October 1919 **Commissioned**: 24 September 1920 **Out of service:** 31 October 1941 **Fate:** Sunk by U-552, 31 October 1941

Class & type: Clemson-class destroyer **Displacement**: 1,190 long tons (1,210 t) **Length**: 314 ft 5 in (95.83 m)

Beam: 31 ft 8 in (9.65 m) **Draft**: 9 ft 4 in (2.84 m) **Installed power**: 26,500 shp(19,800 kW) **Propulsion:** 2 × geared steam turbines 1 × shafts Speed: 35 kn (40 mph; 65 km/h) **Range:** 4,900 nmi(5,600 mi; 9,100 km) @ 15 kn (17 mph; 28 km/h) **Complement:** 159 officers and enlisted

Armament: 4 × 4 in (100 mm) guns 1 × 3 in (76 mm) anti-air-craft gun 12 × 21 in (530 mm) torpedo

"Wow, Dr. Dellinger, this is really fantastic. I didn't know any of this, and I never saw a picture of his ship before. I know my mom hasn't seen any of this. May I keep these?"

"Certainly, Becky. None of this material is classified, although the Navy doesn't make it all that easy to find. This is all very basic; if you give me a week or ten days, I'm sure I can find more detailed information either at the Pentagon or over at the Naval Institute at Annapolis. You can consider being an historian sort of like being on a lifetime scavenger hunt. It's not so much what we find, but the thrill of the hunt that makes this so satisfying. And if we can help someone answer basic questions about family or friends, all the better!"

Navy Historical Center on M Street S.E, at the Washington Navy Yard

CHAPTER 8
FIRST, DO NO HARM

Monday, July 22, 1968 – Washington

While Becky was busy with Dr. Dellinger, Tom and Admiral Tomsen drove the short distance from the Washington Navy Yard to the Naval Annex in Arlington, Virginia. The Navy Annex, which was originally built as a warehouse in 1941, had served as office space for a number of subordinate commands since the Korean War.

After parking and passing through Marine security, they found the suite of the Chief of the Navy Nurse Corps in the easternmost wing of the building. After entering, they were greeted by a young Navy yeoman, and escorted into Captain Conroy's office. The gray haired and stern featured nurse rose to greet them.

After a perfunctory handshake, she gestured to two chairs facing her desk. "Would either of you two gentlemen care for a cup of tea? Mr. Tomsen? Mr. Carpentier?"

"Excuse me, Captain. but it's *Admiral* Tomsen, and this is Lieutenant Commander Carpentier. While it's true that he left the service at the end of World War II, I think he still deserves the courtesy of his title."

Captain Conroy looked at them with suspicion. "You'll have to excuse me, Admiral. I didn't realize that that either of you were still on active duty. It's not often that I have civilians here in my office."

"I'm retired, and we won't detain you long, Captain. LCDR Carpentier is investigating the death of his daughter, and we hoped that you might be able to shed some light on the circumstances."

Captain Conroy rose, and went to the door of her private office. "Yeoman, kindly summons Lieut. Levy and LTJG Miller to my office immediately." While she awaited their arrival, she returned to her desk and, ignoring her visitors, busied herself with paperwork.

It was only a few moments until the two junior officers arrive. Taking seats on an adjacent couch, they waited expectantly.

"What questions have you for me, *Mr.* Carpentier? I've asked Lt. Levy of the Judge Advocate's office, and LTJG Miller of Public Affairs to sit in with us so that we can attend to this matter today. As you can imagine, we are quite busy here."

"I'll get right to the point," said Tom. "My only daughter, LTJG Mary Kay Carpentier was reported as killed in action in December 1966. The only information that I or my family received was that she died as a result of wounds received in combat. Her body was returned to us in a sealed coffin and later cremated. We would consider it a great courtesy if we could learn the exact circumstances of her death."

Captain Conroy turned to LTJG Miller. "Miss Miller, I believe you have some information we can share with Mr. Carpentier."

The young lieutenant removed a single sheet of paper from her folder. She began to read:

"Pursuant to official orders, LTJG Mary Kay Carpentier, NC, USNR was engaged in a Medical Civic Action Program (*MEDCAP*), in support of elements of the First Marine Division at or near the village of Nam O, near Danang, Republic of Vietnam on 13 December 1966 during which she received wounds which later proved to be fatal. Her death at the Naval Support medical unit early in the morning of 14 December 1966 was ruled to be combat-related, and her remains were evacuated to Dover AFB the following morning."

"That is all the information which I am prepared to share with you." said the captain. LTJG Miller will share a copy with you as you leave."

Both Tom Carpentier and Admiral Tomsen sat in stunned disbelief. "Surely, you must have more information than this?"

Lieut. Levy interjected. "I am sorry, gentlemen, but as Captain Conroy has clearly said no other information will be made available to you."

Admiral Tomsen replied angrily, "In nearly 30 years of Naval service I have never seen a *junior officer* react in such a cavalier and manifestly unprofessional manner. Do not think, Captain Conroy, that you have heard the last of this matter. We intend to investigate this further and to get to the bottom of all this."

Captain Conroy arose. "And now, gentlemen, if you will excuse me, I have a very busy schedule. My yeoman will show you out. Good day."

As they left the office in silent disbelief, Tomsen turned to Tom. "Can you believe that? Who the hell does she think she is? Did you did you notice her uniform? Lots of ribbons there, but nothing indicating any combat experience anywhere. Distinguished Service Medal, Meritorious Unit Commendation Award and a couple of Navy Unit Commendations. Oh, yeah, and a National Service Defense Medal and enough Good Conduct

Medals to sink a steamship: a real warrior, that one. She appears to have come up the ladder solely through administrative positions. Not a lot of ticket punching among our friends in the Navy Nurse Corps, I would imagine."

Tom Carpentier just shook his head sadly. He held the single sheet of typewritten information in his hand. "I was going to share this with my wife and family. But not now. I'm ashamed that this is how the Navy treats anyone, let alone a senior retired officer."

Admiral Tomsen patted him on the shoulder. "Don't you worry for one minute, Tom. I didn't hang around the Navy long enough to make Vice-Admiral without having a few friends in high places. We'll get to the bottom of all this soon enough. Just you hide and watch, shipmate."

On the ride back to Baltimore, Tom and Becky discussed what each of them had learned. Their experiences could not have been more different.

"I think Dr. Dellinger really wants to help us. She had very little notice of our visit, yet she took the time to dig out more information than I had learned in the past 25 years. And she tells me that she thinks she can find a lot more within the next couple of weeks. How did things go for you?"

"It was the exact opposite, Becky. We were stonewalled from the get-go. Captain Conroy pretended that we had taken her by surprise, yet her Public Affairs officer had a prepared write-up with just the basic minimal information. And both the PAO and the lawyer from the Judge Advocate's office appeared to be on standby for her call. It wasn't 90 seconds until both of them were in the office, and it was clear that they had rehearsed what they were going to say and, more importantly, what they weren't going to say. I have to hand it to Tincan, though. He went from 0 to 60 in about two seconds flat. He was a hell of a ship driver, back in our days on destroyers in the North Atlantic, after he got over his initial nervousness.

He's now picked up some real skills as a bureaucratic in-fighter too, I can see."

"Well, Dr. Dellinger said that they would call us when they have some new information. I think, if it's okay with you, I'm going to run up and see my family this weekend. I'll take the photograph and the information she gave me for my mom to look at. I'm really confident that we're going to learn some new things that will put my dad's death in context."

Tom continued. "You know, if it weren't for Admiral Tomsen I would be very discouraged at this point. It's clear to me that something happened, and it probably was embarrassing to the Navy. As an outsider, I wouldn't have had a snowball's chance in hell of breaking through their 'Blue Wall of Silence' but if anyone can, it's our friend Tincan."

Becky leaned over and put her head on Tom's shoulder. "God, Tom. I'm awfully tired. All I wanted to do on the Fourth of July was support the pacifist view on Vietnam. This has really been the most hectic couple weeks I can remember."

Tom reached over with his right hand and took Becky's hand in his. "Me too, kiddo. We'll get through this together. Just take a nap for a while, and I'll wake you when we're back at the condo."

CHAPTER 9
TO SEE THE SEA

Sunday, July 28, 1968 – Ocean City Md.

Early that Sunday morning, Becky called Tom from a pay phone in Havre de Grace, just inside the Maryland state line.

"Hey Tom, I'm on my way back. I should be at the condo in about an hour."

Right as predicted, he heard of the sounds of a powerful automobile pulled into the condo's parking lot. A few seconds later the condo door opened, and Becky tossed a key ring to the bemused mariner.

"Look what I have! Well, not me exactly, it belongs to my cousin Buddy, but he won't be using it for a couple weeks. He's about to go off on his two-week National Guard training exercises at Fort Indiantown Gap, not far from Harrisburg. Rather than have it sit idle for two weeks, he's letting me drive it. Want to come out and see?"

Tom went outside and admired the brand-new 1969 Ford Maverick, among the first of the new model year to arrive at dealerships. Its metallic paint color could only be described as eye-popping. "What the heck do they call that shade of green? The last time I saw that color it was part of the Northern Lights, up in the Beaufort Sea!"

"Buddy said the dealer called it anti disestablish-mint. Personally, as a nurse, I'd call it baby-poop green, but you know how clinical we nurses can be. Buddy says that all of his friends are envious of the car, but then again most of them are coal miners and drive beat up old pickup trucks. You've got to admit it, though, that boy has a taste for automobiles."

"How fast will it go?" asked Tom.

"Hm, that's exactly the same thing the state trooper asked when he pulled me over. He said 65; I held out for 45 in a 50. But I just batted my eyelashes, and he let me go with a warning. He was a nice fellow; I wish I'd had some donuts to give him."

"But here's my great idea: The weather's perfect, why don't you hop in and we can cruise down to Ocean City. I've been to the Ocean City in New Jersey before but never the one here in Maryland."

Tom thought it over for a minute. "Well, we could, but it would be hard to get a week-end motel reservation on a Sunday, and I got a call on Friday that the Naval Historical Center has some new information for the both of us. We'll see them at 10:30 tomorrow morning. I don't know, Becky..."

"I'm ahead of you there. I've already made reservations and I brought along my swimsuit and suntan lotion and a trashy book to read on the beach. You can sit there and watch all the freighters go by if you want."

"Oh, a little bit of a brat now, are you? Well, let me go toss some things into a bag and let's go, then. It may take a little while to get over there with the weekend traffic but if we leave quickly we should miss the worst of it. Sit down, and grab yourself a cup of coffee, and I'll just be a few minutes. And bring something appropriate to wear to the meeting. We can go directly from Ocean City."

They soon were on their way to Maryland' s premier summer resort. Becky drove, and her encounter with the trooper didn't seem to cramp her style. She may, in fact, have set the land speed record for the route. Before noon, they stopped briefly at a gas station to change clothes and were soon on the smooth white sands facing the Atlantic Ocean. They enjoyed the water, and made frequent excursions back to their beach umbrella and towels to dry off. "Hey, how about slathering some more of that *Bain de Soleil* on me, Tom. I do have a tendency to burn when I'm out in the sun too long."

"I have a better idea," Tom said. "Why don't we take a little break and head up to the boardwalk to grab something to eat. We can kind of cruise around up there for a while until check-in time at the motel. Just exactly where are we staying, anyway?"

"At the Eden-Roc at 20th and the boardwalk. It's supposed to be pretty good."

"That's not far; we're at 24th St. now. Let's go wander around for a while."

Tom and Becky spent the rest of the afternoon exploring the busy seaside town. They made their way down to Trimper's amusement piers at the south end of the beach and Tom purchased enough tickets so they could experience each of the 'grown-up' amusements at least once. Becky was especially captivated by the antique carousel, built in 1912. "Oh Tom, let's go ride it again and again! I really do enjoy merry-go-rounds!"

"You're nothing but a big kid, do you know that, Nurse Franks?" Tom laughed, as he checked his watch. "Wow, it's getting near six. Time flies when you're having fun, but maybe we ought to go see about the motel. At the height of the summer season I don't think they'll hold a room much past check-in time." They began to walk steadily toward 20th St.

"The room is in my name Tom, and it's on my credit card. It's my gift to you for everything you've done for me since that disaster on the piers at Philadelphia. My mom and her family were really excited about seeing the information about the *Reuben James*, and even more excited to think that Dr. Dellinger may be able to find even more. I really can't thank you enough."

They arrived at the motel, and checked in. Their room was on the second floor, at the very front of the motel and had an excellent view of the beach and the sea beyond. Becky opened the door and Tom followed her in.

Oh, I see we're in the same room. How are we going to manage that?" Tom asked.

"Er, I do see two beds here, sailor. You're still a married man, aren't you, Tom?"

"And Catholic, too, more or less. Probably less," Tom laughed.

"I used to collect those little nun dolls when I was just a kid. I'm saving myself till marriage, or at least that's what I tell my mom."

"Well, you can grab the first shower then, if you want. Together, we probably have enough sand on us to fill a sandbag, and if this motel is like any other at the shore, the supply of hot water is only a trickle. I'll get the second shower, and then we can go grab some chow."

"Grab some chow! Nobody is going to mistake you for a civilian, Tom! Okay, no peeking, now."

After they cleaned up, they wandered back to the boardwalk and stopped at A greasy spoon, close to their motel. The lines were long, and they chose to stand at the bar for their "seafood medley," essentially anything the kitchen had left late on a Sunday night. But what they did have made up in quantity what it may have lacked in quality, and they returned, satiated and tired, to a rocky night's sleep before their early start the next day.

They both tossed and turned throughout the night. The sea food medley seemed to feature listeria with just a taste of ptomaine. Their scheduled 6:00 wake-up call came at 6:45 but, after quick showers, they were on the road to Washington by 7:30.

"Well, I don't know about you, Tom, but I'm famished now. A night like that kind of takes it out of you, doesn't it?"

"It does indeed. I don't think I've felt worse in years. Want to stop and get some real breakfast? We've got plenty of time, it's less than an hour from here to Washington."

Becky nodded. "Works for me."

"Great. I know a good fast Hot Shoppe on the road into the district. Think you can make it till then?"

Becky continued to drive, and they soon reached the Hot Shoppe on New York Ave. They both ordered large breakfasts. Tom had the Number One country breakfast of griddle cakes, syrup, sausage and coffee while Becky had the Number Ten consisting of French toast, honey, crisp bacon and a large glass of milk. All in all, it was a pretty good start after a not-so-good night.

After eating, they continued to the Washington Navy Yard. "Do you think we're really are going to learn something new?" Becky asked hopefully. "My mom will be so happy if she can learn more about what happened to my dad on the *Reuben James*."

71

"Well, Admiral Tomsen's secretary said that Dr. Dellinger had some things for us. She also said that the admiral would be late in joining us. He has a telephone call scheduled with the Chief of Naval Operations. Even for a retired Vice Admiral, that will take precedence over just about everything."

They arrived at their destination, and were escorted into a conference room. Dr. Dellinger soon joined them.

"Well, it's amazing what you can find when you go looking. I have a number of items here. Let's get started. I think the boss will want to join us as soon as he is finished with his phone call."

She opened a manila folder, and handed a small stack of pages to Tom and to Becky. There were extra copies, no doubt for her own use and for the admiral when he finally arrived. She allowed a couple of minutes, to let them review the messages. "The first is a report from the convoy escort commander" she began.

CHAPTER 10
ESCORT REPORTS

Monday, July 29, 1968 Washington

U.S.S BENSON (421),
Boston, Massachusetts
26 November 1941

FB13/A 4-3
Serial 31
S-E-C-R-E-T

From: COMMANDER. Task Unit 4.1.3
To: COMMANDER Task Force Four

Subject: Report of Escort Operations (HX156)

References:
(a.) CT.F. 4 Secret letter, Serial 00120 of- 10-25-41
(b.) C.T.U. 4.1.3 Serial 23 of 11-3-411.

1. In accordance with paragraph 4 of reference (a) the following data are submitted covering escort operations with Hypo X-ray convoy 156.

GENERAL

1. 44 ships on departure, 42 ships at MOMP. The two stragglers were met while in route from the MOMP to Iceland and given position of convoy.

2. One ship, ANCYLUS dropped astern of convoy each night regaining position at daybreak. This vessel's actions created suspicion and possibility exists that she may have been transmitting radio bearings from the convoy. Noteworthy is the fact that on the night Reuben James was sunk, ANCYLUS was farther astern than usual.

3. Conduct in station keeping, signaling, and darkened ship was satisfactory.

4. Weather conditions good with the exception of two days of very rough seas and extremely low barometer.

5. Air escort only on paper. It is noteworthy that shortly after the British took over the convoy at MOMP, an English plane arrived.

6. Considerable difficulty was encountered contacting relief escort forces at MOMP due to error in escort order of Latitude of one secret position. Eventually error was discovered and the meeting point was transmitted to the British escort commander at his request

as Latitude and Longitude rather than bearing and distance from secret point.

B. SUBMARINE ATTACK

A complete account of the submarine attack and sinking of the USS REUBEN JAMES is contained in reference (b). Concise summary will be repeated as a matter of record.

1. Submarine torpedo attack at 0640 O.C.T. morning of October 31, 1941.

2. The sea was moderate, winds force 3, visibility hazy bu approximately 1/2 to 1 miles in early twilight.

3. Sound conditions only fair as contacts over 1000 yards misleading and not true.

4. Locations of Escorts

```
BENSON                                          JONES
2000                                            2000
YDS                                             YDS
0                                               0
---------------------------------------------------------
                      :
                     :              ^^           :
                                                direct.
                    :                           of
                   :        CONVOY    |  travel
                    :
-----------------------------------------------|----------
TARBELL                                | R. JAMES
2000 YDS                               | 2000 YDS
   0                                       0


                    NIBLACK
                       0
```

5. Convoy speed 8.8 knots. Because of reduced visibility and in order to remain in contact with convoy, escorts with the exception of NIBLACK, not patrolling.

6. Torpedo believed fired from starboard side of convoy.

7. NIBLACK, only radar equipped ship, patrolling astern of convoy. Picked up no contacts. BENSON and TARBELL were ordered to rejoin convoy while remained NIBLACK to aid BENSON. BENSON picked up second contact and fired another standard pattern. NIBLACK passed over area of BENSON attacks and reported small streams of

oil on surface, but gained no contacts. At 0743 in same area BENSON picked up another doubtful contact close aboard and dropped one charge. Echo believed probably due to our ships wake. Escort RUBEN JAMES stationed 2000 yards on port beam of rear ship of the left flank column.

8. No air escorts present.

9. Convoy turned 20° to starboard by emergency turn signal returning to base course one half hour later.

10. NIBLACK and H.P. JONES ordered to rescue survivors, one ship rescuing at steerage way speed while the other ship made sound searches in the vicinity. All living survivors believed rescued.

C. COUNTER ATTACK MEASURES.

1. Operation order contained illumination proce- dures covering entire horizon around convoy. On night of October 31, NIBLACK illuminated suspicious vessel while tracking down a direction finder bearing. Target after illumination identified as English Corvette acting as escort but considerably off station.

2. In mid afternoon, October 31, English Corvette joined convoy. On joining they reported sight contact with two submarines about but submerged and were not damaged nor located.

3. (a.) At 1845, October 25, H. P. JONES made depth charge attack on port side of convoy. No echo could be obtained

by echo ranging, but chattering effect and "whistle effect" noticeable. All indications confirmed possibility of a submarine. H. P. JONES proceeded to the attack and as second charge was dropped a school of porpoises was seen under bow. Cease firing was ordered as third charges were dropped.

(b.) At 0910 on October 29, H.P. JONES picked up an echo on the port bow of convoy, range 1800 yards. Proceeded to make embarrassing attack at 20 knots dropping 3–600 pound charges. Did not regain contact and rejoin formation at 0930.

c. REUBEN JAMES was sunk at 0540 October 31. NIBLACK and H. P. JONES were ordered to rescue survivors astern of convoy as TARBELL and BENSON remained with convoy. TARBELL stationed on starboard flank, then moving from starboard bow to port flank. En-route across the head of the convoy, BENSON picked up contacts ahead of convoy. BENSON ordered to make embarrassing attack and proceeded at 25 kn. BENSON fired 3–600 pound charges and fired "Y" gun. BENSON continued to port side of convoy and at 0600 picked up sound contact on U.S.S BENSON (421), on port beam of convoy. Distance about 4000 yards. An embarrassing attack was made firing 3–600 pound charges and "Y" gun. BENSON turned sharply to left to regain contact and soon picked up what probably was the same contact, distance 300 yards proceeding to attack dropping 3–600 pound charges and firing "Y" gun. Contact was not regained and BENSON ordered to close convoy and take station on port flank. At about 0630 TARBELL reported sound contact on starboard bow of convoy and made embarrassing attack with standard pattern. Contact was not regained and TARBELL remained on station on starboard flank.

d. While en route from MOMP to Iceland morning of November 2, TARBELL picked up contact on starboard quarter of convoy and proceeded with an embarrassing attack. NIBLACK ordered astern to aid in search and attack. No contacts regained. As two ships were returning to station, BENSON at 0710 heard propeller noises bearing astern of convoy. BENSON turned to attack and commenced "pinging" target. At 0718 BENSON reported torpedo wake passing under ship from same direction as bearing of contact, range of sound contact about 1400 yards. BENSON continued attack and at 0725 dropped 3-600 pound charges and fired "Y" gun. NIBLACK and TARBELL at this time approached vicinity of BENSON and TARBELL was ordered to rejoin convoy while remained with NIBLACK to aid BENSON. BENSON picked up second contact and fired another standard pattern. NIBLACK passed over area of BENSON attacks and reported small streams of oil on surface, but gained no contacts. At 0743 in same area BENSON picked up another doubtful contact close aboard and dropped one charge. Echo believed probably due to our ships wake.

2. At 0915 BENSON and NIBLACK rejoin convoy after searching area of contact.

3. H. P. JONES picked up contact on port quarter of convoy and made embarrassing attack. Contact not regained and ship ordered to rejoin at 1142.

4. Radar used continuously; no contacts reported.

5. No record of depth charge patterns. It is the policy of this task unit to fire patterns vertically as well as horizontally, various patterns being used to meet the conditions of each attack.

6. Continuous D/F watches were maintained. During nights cross bearings were taken of all stations appearing close. The middle frequency band (250–550 kcs) was used almost exclusively with frequencies in the neighborhood of 260 to 300 kcs used most frequently.

7. Times are recorded in sub paragraph 3 above. Courses were too varied to enumerate. In following up sound contacts with frequent change of course. Speeds for all attacks 14–15 knots with exceptions as noted in paragraph 3 above.

8. No air escorts at any time.

9. All attacks made with weather conditions good, seas moderate. Rescue work was carried out by NIBLACK and H.P. JONES with one ship making sound search while circling rescue ship. The rescuing ship steamed at steerage way speeds while maintaining a sound watch.

2. Same as (two) of other.

D. It is felt that all the depth charge attacks were carried out with the best procedures possible in each instance. That charge attacks by BENSON and TARBELL during the morning of October 31 may have prevented additional attacks on convoys. Other depth charge attacks, if

actually made on submarine contacts prevented additional possible submarine attacks on convoys.

RB Webb
R. B. Webb

Copy to:
C.N.O.
Cinclant
C.T.U. 4.1.3

Dr. Dellinger remarked: "Unfortunately, an additional page of this report was damaged during microfilming. It relates how the base at Hvalfjordur, Iceland received the news of the sinking, and how two additional destroyers were dispatched within ninety minutes to assist. ORP Dranchek, a Polish destroyer under the command of Kaptain Romuald Nałęcz-Tymiński, along with USS John King sped to the scene and spent four days harassing the wolf-pack which had attacked HX-156. Six other Polish Destroyers, with mixed crews of Slavs from various occupied countries were valued additions to the British-led groups as well."

United States Atlantic Fleet
SUPPORT FORCE
US S Prairie, Flagship

S-E-C-R-E-T   Care Of Postmaster, New York, NY

DEC 11, 1941

FIRST ENDORSEMENT to
C.T.U. 4.1.3 FB13/A4-3 (31)
of November 26, 1941.

From: Commander, Task Force FOUR.
To: The Chief Of Naval Operations,
            (Director Of Fleet Training).
Via: Commander-in-Chief U.S. Atlantic Fleet

SUBJECT: Report of Escort Operations-Convoy Hx-156.

1. As Task Unit 4.1.3 is the unit which included the USS
REUBEN JAMES at the time of her sinking, this report is
of particular interest. The loss of the REUBEN JAMES and
the rescue of survivors has been previously reported
in other correspondence and no further comment will be
made herein.

2. The suspicion actions of the ship ANCYLUS mentioned
in paragraph 1-A-2 of the basic letter are of interest.
Discussion of this matter with the task unit commander
indicates no suspicion was held during conduct of the
escort operation but thought on the matter since then
has raised the suspicion in his mind. This ship was

loaded with high octane gasoline originally intended for Russian consumption but which later was diverted to an English port. It is recommended that the Chief of Naval Operations take such steps as may be practical to investigate the ANCYLUS as a possible source of information to AXIS submarines.

3. During the escort of this convoy, charges were dropped in the nine attacks and an established total of forty-nine charges were expended. Eight of the attacks were emergency attacks and only one a collaborative attack. Three of these attacks were very probably on non-submarine contacts. The only deliberate attacks were by the USS BENSON commencing at 0725, November 2, 1941, during which a torpedo from the direction of the sound contact passed under the ship. Officers of the BENSON were convinced that this was a torpedo and not the wake of a fish. After the two attacks were made by the BENSON small streams of oil were noted on the surface but the personnel of the BENSON and of the NIBLACK were not certain as to the sources of this oil and believed it might have been from one of the surface ships. An organized search only lasting nearly 2 hours failed to disclose any further sound contacts or other information regarding the presence of a submarine.

4. The stationing and instructions for patrolling by the ships of this escort unit have been corrected. The question of patrolling stations at night is a difficult one as it frequently involves the use of extra fuel which can ill be spared. The safety of the escort vessels themselves depends in large degree on active patrolling of stations and the success of convoy operations

calls for active and aggressive patrolling. When the older destroyers have completed the contemplated alterations of the removal of a boiler and installation of additional fuel tanks it is expected that more energetic patrolling of stations under all conditions shall be possible.

5. The stationing of the USS NIBLACK, which was the only vessel equipped with radar, at the rear of the convoy is open to discussion. Actually NIBLACK patrolled at a relatively high speed across the Stern and quarters of the convoy and in these patrols her radar covered the whole rear of the convoy. If attack from both quarters was likely, this use of the NIBLACK was sound. When more radars are available it will be possible to station vessels so equipped on the flanks of the convoy.

6. Little or no success was obtained by the taking of direction finder bearings in this operation but it is believed that this effort to locate the enemy must be continued.

L.E. DENFIELD
L.E. DENFIELD
Chief of Staff

Copy to:

84

United States Atlantic Fleet
SUPPORT FORCE
US S Prairie, Flagship

S-E-C-R-E-   Care Of Postmaster, New York, NY

26 Dec, 1941

SECOND ENDORSEMENT to
C.T.U. 4.1.3 FB13/A4-3 (31)
of November 26, 1941.

From: Commander-in-Chief U.S. Atlantic Fleet
To: The Chief Of Naval Operations,
            (Director Of Fleet Training).

SUBJECT: Report Of Escort Operations-Convoy HX-156.

1. Forwarded, concurring in the recommendations made
   in paragraph 2 o the first endorsement, that steps be
   taken, as practicable, to instigate the ANCYLUS as a
   possible source of information to AXIS submarines.

2. Transmission of this letter by registered mail
   within the continental limits of the United States
   is authorized.

H.R. Stark

CHAPTER 11
BUT WHAT DOES IT MEAN?

Monday, July 29, 1968 Washington

While Tom and Becky read silently, Admiral Tomsen slipped into the room.

"This stuff is really astounding," exclaimed Tom. "I knew Bob Webb when he was XO of the *Niblack,* back in the early days of the war. Man, I've got to tell you, seeing this with his original signature really brings back some memories."

"It's really something, isn't it?" remarked Tomsen. "You can disregard the secret stamps all over these three messages; they were all declassified after 21 years. That was back around '62 or '63, I think. But it certainly gives you an idea as to the basic facts of what happened that morning, at least from the perspective of the guys who were there."

"I feel like I ought to raise my hand before I speak," Becky said half in jest. "I'm not sure what all this means. What is an embarrassing attack? And who or what is MOMP?"

"Well, I think if you are a submariner, and somebody is dropping depth-charges on your roof, you would be somewhat embarrassed," replied Tomsen. "But that's really an archaic usage that was prevalent back in the days of the neutrality patrol. We had to be cautious about how we portrayed our activities in regard to the convoys back then. We worked under the fiction that we were just trying to get those U-boats to the surface. In reality, we'd have been quite happy to blow them to kingdom come. And MOMP is just Navy shorthand for Mid-Ocean-Meeting-Point, where responsibility for the convoy transferred from the western to eastern escorts."

They all sat silently re-reading and absorbing the material. "May I ask where you got this?" Becky inquired.

"It's all on microfilm out at the national records storage facility near Rockville," responded Dr. Dellinger. "I don't know how many millions of documents they have there, but they have materials going back to Revolutionary War times, and the files are fairly easy to locate when you know what you are looking for. It didn't take me much longer than an hour to get these."

Admiral Tomsen interjected. "The important thing is to try to understand what they all mean. Those guys on escort duty were all part of Commander, Task Unit 4.1.3. Their home port was at Portland, but they were all based at Argentia, so this was an out-bound trip for them. On the morning of October 31, the weather was good, and the winds were light. It appears from the diagram, that they were steaming in a standard convoy escort formation. The German sub was to the north of the track of the convoy. It was just a little bit before local sunrise, and the *Reuben James* would have been on the starboard side of the convoy as it moved north by northeast. It would have been almost impossible, and completely unlikely, that the sub skipper would have been able to identify the nationalities of the escorts. I would be very doubtful that he even knew that there were American warships anywhere near him. From what I know of the history of that period, Herr Hitler would have been furious. He had given clear and direct orders not to engage the United States until he had attended to his Eastern front. I don't think I would have liked to have been that sub skipper when he got back to Germany."

"The admiral is right, Becky," Tom continued. "I was in Newfoundland during that time. The U-boats would scatter if they thought they had any Yankee warships anywhere near them. We had one or two incidents – the *USS Kearny* and the *USS Greer* come to mind – but given the massive number of merchant ships and the relatively large numbers of British and Canadian escorts all in a relatively restricted set of sea lanes, it really was a relatively minor contribution on our part."

"So do you mean that the Germans didn't really intend to sink my father's ship?" She asked.

"You never can tell what a sub skipper is thinking," Tom replied. "In four years of chasing subs all around the North Atlantic, you could develop an idea of what their tactics were. If you and they survived long enough, you would almost develop a sense as to what the other guy was thinking. But the fog of war is called just that for a reason. We can all sit in this conference room and dissect what may have happened, and why it may have happened. But, trust me, no one who was not there at the time can ever be certain. But, to answer your question directly, Becky, yes. I can't imagine that the U-boat commander knew he was firing his torpedoes at a neutral ship," Tom concluded.

"What about this ship, the Ancylus, that is mentioned in both the original report and the first endorsement?" asked Becky.

"Well, not to denigrate Bob Webb, but I think he may be grasping at straws on this one. I don't know about that particular ship or that instance, but I never escorted a convoy that didn't have some ships' captains acting squirrelly," continued Admiral Tomsen. "There's just something about merchant captains that make you question their sanity sometimes," he said, looking squarely at Tom and smiling.

"Yeah, crazy like a fox!" replied Tom. "Imagine you're the skipper of a beat-up old tramp steamer, which can barely keep up with even a slow convoy. Add to that an escort commander who keeps zigzagging, throw in complete radio silence, and total blackout conditions so that you can't see the ships in front of you, behind you or off to either side, and you begin to wonder if you wouldn't be a lot safer somewhere else. We used to call it 'fear of the dark' – a merchant ship skipper would drop back a couple of miles and proceed along in the wake of the convoy. Personally, we all knew what he was up to. He figured that if the convoy got hit at night, the Wolfpack would logically concentrate on the target rich environment, and as soon as the fireworks began, our straggler would change course and get the hell out of there as quickly as he could. No, I think Bob Webb was grasping at straws on that one!"

Dr. Dellinger smiled. "It certainly is great having two subject matter experts on anti-submarine warfare tactics in the last war here with us. But I really need to visit someplace where you two sailors can't go. Becky, would you like to tag along?"

As both women departed for the ladies room, Admiral Tomsen came to sit beside Tom. "I just got off the phone with Admiral Moore. He was responding to a note that I sent him last week about your situation. He was not happy to hear about our run-in with the Wicked Witch of the West, or however she is portraying herself this week. He thinks she only has a couple more months until she retires. I don't think he wants to rock the boat with her now, though. He'll let her ride off into the sunset on her dragon and get someone more amenable to replace her."

"The other thing that he mentioned is that he is planning a trip to Vietnam for early next month. He expects to be in-country for about three weeks, and will spend several days at Camp Tien Sha in Danang. The most important thing he told me is that he will be accompanied by the Master Chief Petty Officer of the Navy, Delbert White and the Sergeant Major of the Marine Corps, Herb Sauer. Both of those guys have nearly 30 years service and are highly regarded by the troops. I outlined your concerns about your daughter, and he promised to set both men loose to see what they can find. No guarantees, but he did say that he would communicate with me by secure 'back channel' anything they discover. Personally, I can't see a better way to get to the bottom of this. It's clear that the JAG and PAO teams are doing a full blown cover-up on this on behalf of the Nurse Corps."

"Tincan, I can't thank you enough for your involvement in all this. I literally had nowhere else to turn; being a Navy veteran and having a dime will get you a cup of coffee these days. How quickly they seem to forget."

Dr. Dellinger and Becky returned, giggling. Adm. Tomsen remarked in a falsetto, "Oh Tom, shall we go together and have a tinkle?" Everyone laughed.

Dr. Dellinger resumed. "Well, I have some more information to share with you all. On the way back from the records storage facility, I stopped off at the Library of Congress and picked up some reprints of *New York Times* articles from the period. I've always felt that the *New York Times* is the gold standard of reporting, and anything of interest is better covered there than almost anywhere else. Why don't you take these with you, and read them at your leisure. Over the next few days, I'm going to get a message out to Cuxhaven, and see what the Germans have in their archives that may help us. We don't even know the account of the sinking from their perspective. We believe it was a submarine, but we don't know which one nor who the skipper might have been. But they have an excellent archive near Kiel, and it's been my experience that they are always happy to assist."

"That's really kind of you, Dr. Annie." Becky concluded. "You've certainly given us a good starting point. But I don't think we should take up more of your valuable time today. Tom, are you ready to go?"

"Yes, I think so. You have been extraordinarily helpful on both of these matters we've been discussing, Admiral and Doctor. Give me a call if you have anything new, and I will be down here the next morning."

CHAPTER 12
ALL THE NEWS THAT'S FIT TO PRINT

Monday, July 29, 1968 Baltimore

When they reached the parking lot, Becky tossed Tom the keys to the Maverick. "Why don't you drive us back, Tom? I'll take a look at some of these press clippings that Dr. Dellinger gave us. There must be 20 or more of in the folder."

"No problem. We should be back in Baltimore in an hour or so, do you want to stop somewhere for a late lunch?"

"Sure, as long as it's not a crab restaurant! I love crab, but I think that's the only thing I've ever seen on a menu in Baltimore."

"Oh, there are plenty of good places, I'm sure. By the way, what were you and Dr. Dellinger giggling about when you came back to the conference room?"

Becky laughed. "You know, for an old gal, she's sharp as can be. My mom would say she's so sharp she'd cut herself. She'd be minding mice at a crossroads, as they'd say up home. Anyway, when we went to the ladies room, there was no one else in there. She grabbed a stall, and I took one on the other end of the row. That's what we ladies do, if you didn't know. Well, I suppose the crab we had last night had affected my system somehow. As I sat down on the bowl, I let out the longest and loudest toot that I think I've ever had. Well, not a second or two later I heard an answering toot coming from the other end of the row. It was almost like harmony, and I started laughing so hard, and she started laughing so hard that for a moment neither one of us could attend to the reason why we were there in the first place. And then she said *Gladys Knight and the Poops!* and we both cracked up. It was the funniest thing I've heard in my life, and when we came out of the stalls both of us were laughing so hard that we can hardly fix our makeup or wash our hands. And we were still giggling when we got back into the meeting!"

Tom just shook his head. "I can't imagine guys doing something like that, at least any over the age of 12 or so. So that's why women always go to the restroom in pairs."

Tom swung out into traffic, and was soon on a I-95 heading toward Baltimore. Becky opened the files and attempted to read. "I don't think this is going to work, Tom. These pages are copied from microfilm, and the printing is very faint. Maybe it will be better to do this when we get home."

Tom caught the reference to 'home' but said nothing. Becky closed her eyes and nodded off. They soon reached Baltimore, and Tom drove to the Lexington Market, where he gently shook Becky awake. "We're on North Paca Street, right by Faidley's restaurant. While it's a seafood house, the selection is excellent and you won't be limited to crab meat. I'm sorry if this destroys your future in the entertainment business, but I think you'll like it."

They were seated quickly, and both ordered. Tom had baked codfish and new potatoes, and Becky ordered the house salad and iced tea. "I would've had the fish, but I was afraid it would give me a *haddock*," Becky joked.

"Every time I heard that pun in Newfoundland, I had to stop and *mullet* over," Tom replied. Both laughed.

94

"Tell me more about your family, Tom. How did you meet your wife, and what's life like for them in Newfoundland?"

"Well, I was stationed at Argentia, on the south coast of the island, from the spring of 1941 onward. I had come off a destroyer, and was the officer-in-charge of a radio station there. Loretta taught in the little parochial school outside the gate, and we actually met at a parish social, if you can believe that. We hit it off, and got married the next spring."

"Mary Kay, our only child, was born in late 1942. She would be 26, almost 27 now. I didn't see much of her or her mom after they left Louisiana in 1948. They went back to live with her family in St. John's. I got up there to see them as often as I could, but not nearly as often as I would have liked. Birthdays, graduations, all the little events of life – I wasn't there to participate."

"That must have been terrible, Tom. Tell me, did you still love her?"

"Yes, I loved her when we married, I loved her then and I love her now. Newfoundlanders understand that men sometimes must go to sea for months on end. No one in her family really thought it was unusual. Her father, her grandfather and all of her uncles were offshore fishermen. They went out in trawlers and longliners, and if they came ashore, often enough it would be on the other side of the island, or even in Nova Scotia or New Brunswick. And it's been that way for hundreds of years. But I did get there when I could, and yes, we still considered ourselves married – with everything that that entails."

"It was really sort of funny, in a way. All of her aunts and friends used to tease her about when we would have another child. But we thought, under the conditions, that that would be the wrong thing to do. Now, both of us regret that decision."

"And how did your daughter take this?"

"She was young enough when they returned to St. John's that it all seemed normal to her. I did get up there enough that she knew I was her daddy and that she always looked forward to the times when I was there. And sometimes I was able to stay for a couple months at a time."

They both enjoyed their meals and, after lingering over coffee, paid the check and continued their drive back to the condo. After cleaning up and changing clothes, Becky spread the contents of the two bulging manila envelopes on the dining room table.

"There must be two dozen clippings in each of these envelopes. One envelope is for you, and the other for me, but Dr. Annie even stapled the packets together and numbered each clipping in the upper right-hand corner. She certainly is hyper-organized. Shall we start with the first clipping?"

Tom nodded.

RUBEN JAMES HIT
First American Warship Lost In War
Torpedoed West Of Iceland
The Details Of Sinking And Fate Of Rest Of Crew
Are Not Yet Known
By Charles Hurd
Special To The New York Times

Washington, October 31--the United States lost its first warship in the Battle of the Atlantic when the destroyer Reuben James was torpedoed and sunk last night west of Iceland while on convoy duty, the Navy announced today

The Navy later announced that 44 members of the crew had been rescued. It was without a word however, as to the fate of the other 120 officers and men which made up her complement.

The text of the Navy's second announcement read:

"The Navy department has received a report that 44 members of the crew of the USS Reuben James have been rescued. The survivors who have been accounted for are all enlisted men. The Navy department has no further information at this time, but additional details will be released when received."

The meager reports on the sinking were believed to be due to the fact that radio silence for all but the most urgent messages is an inviolate rule of ships serving on the Atlantic patrol. The flashing of detailed messages by wireless serves in effect as a beacon to notify other enemy vessels where to find our ships which sent them out.

News of the sinking of the Reuben James created an immediate stir in Washington, on Capitol Hill particularly, but President Roosevelt sounded a conservative note in a press conference when he stated that they sinking did not change any aspect of the international position of the United States.

The sinking of the Reuben James presented only the result which might have attended torpedo attacks on two other destroyers which recently have engaged German submarines. The destroyer Greer, first to figure in such an incident, escaped without being hit. The destroyer Kearny was hit by one of three torpedoes launched simultaneously and survived, but with the loss of 11 members of her crew.

The Kearny was a new destroyer, which proved the strength of its type in surviving a torpedo hit. The Reuben James, a 21-year-old member of the "tin can" fleet, met the fate that all sailors long have agreed a destroyer faced if hit by a torpedo.

The Reuben James is believed to have gone down in the area where the other American destroyers were attacked. The Navy's first announcement of the sinking was as follows:

"The Navy department announced that the United States destroyer Reuben James was sunk by a torpedo during the night of October 31 while escorting a convoy in the North Atlantic, west of Iceland. The commanding officer is Lieut. Cmdr. H. L. Edwards, United States Navy. No further details are available at this time will but will be released when received."

If the engagement which cost the Reuben James occurred in the place where the previous attacks were made the vessel or vessels which witnessed and report its sinking presumably would be some hundred of miles from land, whether Iceland or Newfoundland, and perhaps a day or more would elapse before they could fully determine who survived and reached a safe place from which to relate further news.

It seemed probable to informed persons here acquainted with the fleet operations and with the destroyer itself (in the absence of official comment), that the Reuben James was probably sunk in a general engagement rather than in single combat with a submarine.

American destroyers, like the British ones, are equipped with various devices which make it virtually impossible for a single submarine to catch a destroyer unaware and approach within torpedoing distance. It appears probable, therefore, that a pack of submarines was involved in this attack. By the same token, in view of the system of naval operation, it is probable that other destroyers were on the scene in addition to the Reuben James and there is at least an even chance that the submarine which won this victory did not long survive it.

This corresponded last summer traversed the route along which the Reuben James presumably was sunk while cruising with a task force of the Atlantic Fleet, convoying a group of transports to Iceland.

The Reuben James was one of a squadron of destroyers which did wide-ranging patrol as a screen for the transports and larger ships making up the convoy.

On the summer cruise the days in the northern Atlantic were 20 hours along. Now they are proportionately shorter, and the long dark hours make the work of submarines easier and that of convoy escorts proportionately difficult.

The Reuben James was a low-lying, four,-stack destroyer of the long familiar type, identical in design to the 50 destroyers traded to Great Britain under the Lend Lease program. Like her sister ships, the tall stacks shown in photographs had been cut down to stubs, so that it presented racy lines in profile as it and the other destroyers zigzagged along the predetermined course.

There was more than sufficient life-saving equipment aboard the destroyer if the complement survived to use it. This included two boats, each with a capacity of 24 people, and at least six large balsa rafts, to each of which 25 men could cling. But the waters in that region are very cold.

The Reuben James was commissioned September 24, 1920. It was 314 feet long and had a maximum width of 30 feet. It displaced 1190 tons and was armed with 44-inch naval rifles and a battery of anti-aircraft guns. To this original equipment had been added the modern secret detectors developed in the last two years.

"This news report seems very much like the Navy document that Dr. Dellinger shared with us," Becky remarked.

"No doubt the *New York Times* based this story on the first press releases sent out by the Navy in Washington later that morning," Tom replied. "That would be the procedure that I would expect, anyway." "Let us see what the next story contains. It seems to be from the perspective of some of the 44 men who survived the catastrophe."

MEN DESCRIBE LOSS OF REUBEN JAMES
One Petty Officer Left Led 44 Surviving Enlisted Men To The Rescue Rafts
Attack Was Before Dawn

No Answer Came Again From Breach Then Oil Spread

The missile that ended the career of the destroyer Reuben James and made her the first United States naval vessel to be lost in the present war struck without warning during the early hours of October 31 and cost of lives of all of her officers and all of her petty officers except one who led the 44 enlisted men remaining alive after the blast over the side into three rescue rafts.

The James, her bow demolished, sank about 20 minutes later, as the dawn began to lighten the horizon, the remnants of her crew sighted another United States naval vessel, which effected their rescue.

This account, conveyed among recollections of complete surprise, of darkness, of oil covered, bitterly cold water and of quixotically insignificant episodes, was made yesterday by 43 of the 45 men who survived the sinking, leaving behind 100 officers and men of the World War vintage four-stacked.

Survivors Land In Brooklyn

The survivors arrived at 2:30 PM yesterday at the New York Port of Embarkation, 58th Street, Brooklyn, aboard a United States Maritime Commission transport ship, Alogorab. They were interviewed four and a half hours later at the receiving ship USS Seattle, berthed in the Hudson River at 52nd Street, under supervision of Navy public relations officers.

The two not present at the interview --their names were given only as Tommy Turnbull and Thompson--are being treated for injuries. The officers forbid discussion of their whereabouts.

Naval authorities also forbid the survivors to describe the type of missile that hit the destroyer, but that the Navy Department announced on October 31 that she was torpedoed west of Iceland while on convoy duty.

William Henry Bergstresser, 35 years old, a chief petty officer and machinist mate, upon whose command devolved with the death of the ship's officers was in the forward engine room when the torpedo struck.

A slim, dark haired man of middle height and gray eyes, Chief Bergstresser told the story, as he remembered it, in the luxurious lounge of what formerly was the pier of the Italian Line, while 42 of his men, numbering youths and veterans with three and four hash-marks, lounged about playing the piano and reading the books placed in the room for the men of the Seattle.

Would Like To Go Home

All looked healthy, and spoke of hope for leaves to visit their homes before being reassigned to other ships.

Chief Bergstresser, whose home is in Pittsburgh, Pennsylvania, recalled that a second impact--caused by the explosion of the ship's magazine, which was forward --followed the first. He could not say whether the blow came from port or starboard.

With six other men in the two engine rooms, he went topside to appraise the damage.

"The flow of steam was interrupted, so the lights were eliminated," he said.

The James shook, shivering with a sinking motion, and when he arrived on deck, was "down by the bow."

The whole forward part of the ship was demolished, and the bridge, with its means of signaling by radio and lights, was carried away. Calls to "bridge control" even shouted, brought no response.

The petty officer was informed by Rudolph Kapercz, 28, of Ironwood Michigan, a gunners mate who was on watch at the after anti-aircraft piece, that no officers were saved. Nor did any other survivor of the James ever see or hear of them again. Their quarters were all forward as were those of the petty officers and some of the crew.

Chief Bergstresser, now in command, ordered three of the James' six life rafts thrown overboard, and he and the crew followed. About 20 minutes later, all the rafts were some 100 yards away, and the James went under with an explosion.

In another 20 minutes, rescue appeared in the form of another United States naval vessel. The survivors stayed two days aboard the rescue vessel and then were transferred to another ship. The names of the ships and the whereabouts of the men since the sinking were withheld.

It is expected that the men will be quartered aboard the Seattle until reassignment.

The sinking took place in a calm sea with no wind. Survival of many of those who went over the side was attributed by Chief Bergstresser to an order issued some months ago by the James's master, Lieut. Cmdr. Haywood L. Edwards, that all men have their life belts at hand at all times.

Men Just Felt Alone

When the James went down the men "just felt like they were all alone" Chief Bergstresser said.

"They felt there was something there as long as the ship was floating," he added, "they felt lost when she went down."

One seaman, despite the disaster, had the yen to find out how the water was before going over side. William Westbury, a 30 year old machinist mate first class from Charleston, South Carolina, took off his shoe, and like a Mack Sennett bathing beauty, dipped in his foot. "It was cold," he said.

Joseph Beihl, 21, of Akron Ohio, a throttle man who arrived on the deck barefooted after the torpedo struck said: "I figured at the ship would stay up so I went back and got my shoes." He was wearing them yesterday.

Tom and Becky read through the survivors reports, and Becky sat silently, with tears in her eyes for several minutes. Tom knew that she was imagining the terror that her father had experienced that freezing, pre-dawn morning in the frozen North Atlantic. Finally, he spoke. "If it's any consolation at all, Becky, from what I know of the layout of a Clemson class destroyer, it's most likely that your father, as a machinist's mate second class, was probably amidships or in the forward sections of the *Reuben James* when it went under. And that was a matter of just a couple minutes after the torpedo hit. He did not suffer long, if at all." Becky just sat there, staring into space.

CONGRESSIONAL REACTION
(The New York Times, November 1, 1941)

Sen. Buckley, Democratic floor leader--. It appears that the Nazis are determined to drive us off the seas and I don't believe the American people are ready to be driven off.

Sen. Capper, Republican of Kansas--This apparently brings us closer to a fighting war.

Sen. Gurney, Republican of South Dakota--this clinches the argument for repeal of the neutrality law

Sen. Aiken, Republican of Vermont--President Roosevelt has ordered convoys in spite of his repeated promises and is personally responsible for whatever lives may have been lost.

Sen. Lucas Democrat of Illinois--This is further proof of Hitler's well laid plan and terrorist scheme to drive every ship, regardless of its nationality, out of the sea lanes of the Atlantic.

Sen. Adams, Democrat of Colorado--Once we gave the orders to shoot, it was inevitable that we were going to be shot at. We ought to be minding our own business and not participating in a war.

Rep. Shanley, Democrat of Connecticut--The sinking of the Reuben James will bring realistically to the American people the price we are paying for measures short of war. The tragic consequence of events substantiates Pres. Roosevelt's statement of last year that convoy means shooting and shooting means war. Measures short of war must inevitably lead to war.

Sen. David L Walsh, chairman of the Naval Affairs Committee-- The policy we are pursuing must inevitably lead to sinking and more sinking. The doctrine of freedom of the seas does not permit a country to bring munitions of war to a belligerent without exposing its convoys of munitions to attack.

"This is terrible!" exclaimed Becky. "All these politicians--all they seem to want to do is to blame things on someone else! It's nobody's fault, or maybe it's everybody's fault. You can just see these senators and congressmen jockeying for position. It's disgusting!"

105

"No argument there, Becky. It's like that even today in the Congress. Some guys are blaming everything on Lyndon Johnson while others defend him regardless of how stupid and self-serving many of his decisions have been. You'd think after the last 25 years, we'd have learned something. But we haven't, and I'm not sure we ever will."

---

40 WIVES AT PORTLAND
Special to The New York Times
(published November 2, 1941)

Portland, Maine November 1- Red-eyed and listless after hours of vigil with little sleep, about 40 wives of members of the crew of the destroyer Reuben James, now living in Portland, were anxiously awaiting official word from the Navy Department.

Several wives made individual pleas to the department and to Navy officials here, asking if their husbands were among the known 44 saved.

This Portland base for the North Atlantic patrol, experienced a mild flurry of excitement when a mid-afternoon ringing of church bells gave rise to the rumor that the survivors--or the dead--have been brought here. The bells, however, were for society weddings.

An organization of Navy wives formed to help one another find homes here and maintain contacts, said that it did not have complete records to determine how many of the Reuben James crew live in Portland. Some estimates place the total at 60, or almost half of the crew of 114 men and seven officers, but a later check brought the estimate down to 40.

Mrs. Solon D. Boyd, wife of a machinist mate on the destroyer, tearfully recounted a prediction last week by her husband. "I'm afraid we won't be back this time," he said. Mrs. Boyd declared that the Reuben James seems to have a "holiday jinx" as a year ago on Thanksgiving it ran aground off Key West, Florida. News of its sinking reached her on Halloween.

The destroyer left Portland last Sunday. Mrs. Boyd and her six-year old daughter have been living in Portland for two months.

Also here are Mrs. Catherine Sims, wife of Lloyd E. Sims, first-class water tender from Marinia, Florida; Mrs. Loretta James, wife of V. G. James, a fireman and the wife of William H. Bergstresser, acting chief machinist's mate.

At Stanford, the family of Albeni Doiron awaited word of the fate of Gilbert Doiron, 32, first class petty officer, who visited his parents and twenty-month-old son two weeks ago.

Mrs. Boyd, who has been married for seven years, told reporters that her husband was "to go up for his chief machinist rating on Thursday," according to a letter mailed October 21 in Newfoundland and received here Tuesday.

"I couldn't believe my ears when I heard the news on the radio--I just froze in my chair," she said concerning the sinking. Her daughter recognized the name of her father's ship, and began to cry and could not be consoled. The Boyds are from Birmingham, Alabama, and Boyd is a veteran of 11 years naval service.

Naval officers estimated that several hundred wives of Navy officers and enlisted men are living in this city, as more than twenty-six vessels are making this their home port.

After reading the fourth clips, Becky lost any attempt at self-control. She cried inconsolably. Tom took the story about the wives and children of the men of the *Rubin James* and placed it back in the manila envelope. It was several minutes before Becky regained her composure.

"I think we should stop reading these for a while," he said. Becky nodded. "And I'm not at all sure that you should share this news story with your mom. How do you think she might react?"

She nodded. "There are some other things I need to share with you about my childhood, Tom." He listened attentively.

"When my dad was reported missing and then later declared dead, my mother was devastated. She walked around in a fog for many months; she was completely inaccessible to me and to the rest of her family, even when she was in the same room. Things got better for a while, but she never admitted to herself that he was gone. Then, about four years later when the war ended—well, things really got worse. She always expected that he would walk in the front door again, but when the Japanese surrendered in the fall of 1945, all of her hopes--her rationalizations as they might have been—were dashed."

"I remember it was a terribly warm day in August. Mom was almost manic, she was running around the kitchen and I remember she was making a big gallon pot of bean soup. Navy bean soup. She got dressed in her warmest coat, wrapped me up in a heavy snowsuit and scarf and mittens – it was August, remember – and took me and the pot of bean soup out to the school bus shelter at the end of our road. She was going to wait for dad to come home, and in her delusion, thought that the bean soup and the heavy clothes would help warm him up. Warm him up – after four years he spent in the freezing waters."

"I nearly passed out from the heat. It had to have been at least 85°, and we were out there for several hours. Finally, a neighbor spotted us and came out to see what was going on. By that time, mom was totally incoherent. Thankfully, the neighbor went back inside and called the county. The two sheriffs who came out realized that mom had completely broken with reality. One deputy took her away in the patrol car, while the other waited with me until a welfare-worker showed up. They were both very nice to me, and explained that mom had to go to the hospital for a while. The man from the welfare board took me to an orphanage run by the Sisters of Mercy. I have never heard of a group of women less deserving of the name."

"The man from the welfare office told me I would only be there for a few days. I was eight years old, nearly nine, and I didn't leave the orphanage until after my thirteenth birthday. All of this turmoil, and all my guilt from the day of my dad's death onward, had really messed me up, Tom. I wet the bed almost every night. In the mornings, one of the nuns in charge of the dorm used to come through and check bed sheets. If they were wet, she would make us wear them on our heads in front of everyone, and encourage them to mock us. And each one of those nuns carried a thick black leather strap, split into two tails at the business end. I cannot tell you how many times that strap cracked across my naked backside. We could be whipped for anything: bed wetting, insubordination, not doing our assigned housework, not being reverent and attentive in church, 'forgetting our station,' even attempting to be friendly with the other girls. Four years and seven months, Tom. We were just numbers to them. I nearly forgot my name. Four years and seven months."

Tom moved closer and held her hand. "God, Becky, I am so sorry. I can't even begin to comprehend how bad it was."

"Don't, Tom. Don't sympathize with me. Don't tell me it's all over now. Don't tell me to get on with my life. It's not over now. It continues in my mind every single day. Oh yes, they finally released my mother from the mental hospital and me from the orphanage and we continued with our lives as best we could. But on October 31 1941, my life changed forever, and no one can ever change it back."

CHAPTER 13
THE SHORES OF NEWFOUNDLAND

Wednesday, July 31, 1968 – St. John's NFLD

Tom and Becky both retired early, drained by the emotions of the day. Tom awoke early the next morning and, after a quick shower prepared breakfast. Becky, hearing the commotion from the kitchen of the small condominium entered just as Tom was setting the table.

"Oh, you didn't have to do that. I would be happy to cook for us whenever we're not eating out," Becky said.

"No problem at all," replied Tom. "When I'm alone here I'm usually up and about by 6 AM or so. That's what a life aboard ship can do to you."

"Which destroyers were you on, Tom, back during the war?"

"Well, I first shipped out on the *USS Niblack,* and spent four years on board before being transferred to the Naval Radio Station at Argentia when the base opened in the summer of 1941. I stayed there for a year or so, and then went aboard the *USS Hanlon* as executive officer. We escorted convoys as far east as Iceland, where we met the British destroyers and and corvettes and handed off the convoys to them to be routed through the western approaches to Britain."

"When *Hanlon* went into the yards for some much needed maintenance in late 1943, I was given command of the *USS Dennis N. Terry* and stayed aboard her until the war ended. I actually brought the *Terry* back to the James River reserve fleet and mothballed her as my last trip. I didn't even have a change of command ceremony to mark my departure from the Navy. There were just a couple of civilian yard workers on hand to wave goodbye."

"It must have been terrifying to be out there on a destroyer." Becky remarked. "Were you scared?"

"It's like they say about a lot of things. There were hours of boredom, punctuated by moments of terror."

"Did you ever sink any German submarines or warships?"

Tom sat silently. Finally he spoke. "Yes, we did. We were credited with the sinking of two German submarines when I was aboard *Hanlon*, and the sinking of another in 1944. One of the most interesting things, though, was that we participated in the capture of a German submarine, the U-505 in June of '44. There was a small U.S. aircraft carrier, the *USS Guadalcanal*, skippered by a complete wild man, Captain Daniel V. Gallery, who happened upon the 505 on the surface. He managed to capture the German submarine, and all but one member of their crew alive and began towing it back to Hamilton, Bermuda, which was the closest port with good security to keep the whole incident secret from the Germans. It must have worked! This submarine is now a museum piece in Chicago. You ought to go and see it sometime."

"I'll skip it, thank you. German U- boats are not something I want to be around."

Becky continued. "By the way, Tom, I did look through the rest of those two dozen or so news stories that Dr. Annie gave us. Many of them recount the same facts that we read yesterday, and many others were obituaries of specific sailors who were lost. I think I am going to take the entire envelope full of clips home with me. Whether or not I share them with my mom depends a lot on how she reacts to the things we've learned so far. I think I'm going to head up there today, and I'm planning to stay a while. Why don't you give me a call if we get any new information, and I can be back down here in just a couple hours."

"Well, I'm glad you brought that up. actually. I had originally planned to go back to Newfoundland during this layover. Since it may take a couple of weeks for any information to come from Germany in response to Dr. Dellinger's request, this looks like a good time to go. I'll give you my father-in-law's phone number in St. John's, in case you have any reason to contact me over the next few weeks. Please, please – even if you just need to talk, call me. And as soon as I get any information back from the Naval Historical Center, I'll call you."

Becky departed before lunch, and Tom drove out to BWI airport later that afternoon and purchased a round-trip ticket to St. John's. Departing the following morning via Boston, he arrived on the island later that afternoon. After a warm welcome from his wife and her family, his mother-in-law prepared a traditional Newfoundland 'scoff' of boiled cod tongues, Jig's dinner (boiled cabbage and corned beef) and pease pudding (peas boiled in a linen bag).

As happened every time the prodigal son returned home, the next week or so was chock full of invitations to dinner with Loretta's many relatives, and the occasional 'kitchen-party,' featuring plenty of accordion and fiddle music so beloved by Newfoundlanders. The current hit song, sung by a Newfoundlander named Dick Nolan, was entitled "Aunt Martha's Sheep" and recounted the perhaps apocryphal tale of a mainland-born Mountie, sent to investigate the theft of poor Aunt Martha's favorite animal. After many misadventures, he was tricked into eating the poor beast by some scoundrels who invited him in, saying "Come right in and join us, sir, were having a bit of Moose!"

"That was a funny song, the first 200 times I heard it," Tom remarked to his wife as they drove out to Logy Bay to have dinner with her third cousin, twice removed. "But it is getting a bit old, if I do say so myself."

Tom had brought some notes from Adm. Tomsen and Dr. Dellinger, and one afternoon stopped in at the Crows Nest, a World War II officers club on Water Street. The club had been painstakingly maintained for the past 25 years and any destroyerman or other sailor who wandered in would find the place – up 59 rickety stairs, just as Tom had remembered it –exactly as it was on the day the war ended. Tom looked through much of the memorabilia that had been collected and preserved as a small museum, and copied some records of convoy HX-156 which had been escorted by the *Reuben James* and five other US destroyers. Tom signed the logbook and had a Blue Star beer with the barman, and as he left the club, bowed his head in silent homage to former shipmates, now forever on "Eternal Patrol." As he left, he recalled ruefully that the long outdoor staircase also was required for the trip down. "My God," he thought to himself "how did I ever maneuver this after a long night of drinking with my shipmates? This was probably the most dangerous thing any of us would encounter, and that includes an ocean full of U-boats!"

When he safely reached Water Street, he turned left and walked a few blocks to Campbell's Ships Supply, the oldest and largest ship's chandlers in Newfoundland. Entering, he went immediately to the chart department and obtained several small and large scale charts of the waters between Greenland and Iceland. When he returned to his father-in-law's house, he spotted a note on the kitchen table which read "Tom – Admiral Tomsen called. He has some important news for you. Please call him at your convenience."

Tom looked at his watch. It was 4:30 PM Newfoundland Daylight Time, which was 1 1/2 hours ahead of Eastern Daylight Time in Washington, and Tom knew that Admiral Tomsen would still be in his office. He dialed the phone and was shortly connected with the admiral himself.

"Tom! Don't tell me you're homesick for Newfoundland! Personally, I loved the place and the people more than anywhere I have ever been stationed, but it does get bloody nippy in the winter, though, which starts about July, doesn't it?"

"I still have family here, Tincan. I get back up as often as my schedule will allow. I've eaten more fish and brewis in the last two weeks than most guys would eat in a year, though. What's up?"

"I've got a lot of new information for you. Number one, Dr. Dellinger got a report yesterday from the Germans. According to the ships' log books in the archive there, *Reuben James* was attacked by the U-552. At that time the skipper was none other than the Knight's Cross Holder, Erich Topp. And not only that, she checked his bio and there is an interesting story here. He survived the war, picked up some Swords and Diamonds for his Knight's Cross, and after the war went back to school and became an architect. I don't think they had anything like the G. I. Bill in Germany, so he did it on his own dime or pfennig or whatever. He worked as an architect for several years. When the Bundesmarine was reformed, he went back on active duty and is on active duty still. Not only that, but I'll bet you all the codfish in Newfoundland you don't know what he's been up to, lately."

"You got me on that one, Tincan. Where is he?

"Well, he was right here in Washington with NATO for four years, and now he's chief-of-staff in Bonn. He's one of the good guys now, and has been one for the past 20 years or so."

"Well, everybody's got to be somewhere," Tom remarked. "But I wouldn't have bet on that one."

"But there's more! Dr. Dellinger managed to get the complete logbook for the sixth patrol of the U-552. I have your address in Baltimore; I'll stick it in the US mail and you can take a look when you get home. And here's the really interesting part. I was talking to Captain Yost up at the Naval Institute in Annapolis. Because this is Topp's twilight cruise before he retires, they have invited him to speak to a group of historians on August 22. That's just a couple weeks from now. If you want to come and hear him speak, and can guarantee that your young friend will not do anything to embarrass Topp or the Naval Institute, we can get you into that conference so long as you don't ask any questions or draw attention to yourselves. Do you think you would be interested?"

"I certainly am," replied Tom. "Now as for Becky, I'm not so sure. She's been pretty traumatized by this whole situation and is at home in Pennsylvania now trying to make sense of it all. But I'll certainly ask her."

"Good. I'll put in a tentative okay to the guys in Annapolis, and if we have to cancel, well, no harm-no foul. And now my last piece of hot G2 for you today is that Admiral Moore and his staffers leave for San Diego tomorrow. He'll spend a couple of days there, and then fly out to Hawaii. Ostensibly, he's going to participate in a couple of change of command ceremonies, although knowing the CNO, I bet he will get several rounds of golf in at every stop before finally flying to Vietnam. Once he's in Vietnam, he will head south of Saigon down to where the Riverine forces are working in the Delta. After that, he will head up to I Corps and spend about a two weeks up there before coming back stateside. He's already briefed his two senior enlisted guys about your concerns. So we'll see how things go."

"Tincan, I can't thank you enough for everything you have done. It's been above and beyond the call of duty. Bravo Zulu, shipmate."

"Bravo Zulu, my ass," the admiral replied. If I can't help my first skipper, what the hell is the Navy coming to? Give me a call when you get back, or if I have anything new for you I'll get in touch with you as quickly as I can."

Later that evening, Tom and Loretta dined at the small restaurant inside the Arts and Culture Centre near the campus of the Memorial University of Newfoundland. As they dined, Tom told Loretta about his plans to learn more about the circumstances surrounding Mary Kay's death.

"Why don't you come back to the States with me for a while? I still love you, and I know you love me. Why don't we try to make a go of it again, especially after everything that's happened in the last two years?"

"Oh Tom, you know that I've always loved you. But you know how uncomfortable I was when you were away at sea all the time and how I felt trapped – and that's the best word I can use to describe my feelings – trapped in what was to me an alien culture. And after what your country did to our daughter, there is no way that I could ever be comfortable there again, even for a moment. If it weren't for the support of my family and friends here in Newfoundland, I could not have survived the shock, despair and depression that the United States Navy caused me. I have no idea why it's so important for your country to be fighting in Vietnam. It makes no sense to me, or to most other Canadians either. I'm sorry, Tom. We can remain married as long as we live, and you are always welcome to my home and to my bed. But no, Tom, I will never return to the United States. Never."

Tom understood, and Loretta's reaction was not unexpected. In many ways he felt the same. "Well, I do have to get back down there soon. There are some developments concerning Mary Kay's death that I need to pursue, and I can only do that in person. I promise you, Loretta, that anything I learn I will tell you, regardless of how distressing it may be. You are her mother, after all."

"When do you expect to fly out, Tom?"

"The day after tomorrow. I've already changed my ticket and I can grab a cab from your dad's house out to Torbay airport. I should be ashore in Baltimore for about two more months, and then off at sea again for about six months. I promise to come back up here in the early spring."

Tom left as scheduled, and was back in Baltimore by the late that afternoon. An envelope from the Naval Historical Center was in his mailbox, and when he opened it he found a copy of Erich Topp's deck log for his sixth combat patrol, neatly translated into English by the staff of the U-boat Archives in Cuxhaven-Altenbruch.

After reading the deck logs, he telephoned Becky. "There have been some new developments, and you may want to be here for a meeting in Annapolis in the middle of August. I'll give you all of the details when you get here. There are some decisions you'll have to make. But I think we are getting closer to understanding not only what happened, but why."

She agreed, and Tom picked up Becky when she arrived at Pennsylvania Station. During the the drive back to the condo he explained to her what he had learned so far and what he expected they might still learn.

"We now know the name the submarine that sunk your father's ship. It was the U-552, commanded by a fellow named Erich Topp. He was the equivalent of a lieutenant commander in the German U-boat service at the time, and went on to a long career in the West German Navy. He even was their delegate to NATO, right here in Washington, a few years ago. He's now the Chief of Staff of the West German Navy, and apparently is getting ready to retire. He's been invited back to the Naval Institute at Annapolis to discuss his experiences over the past 30 years or so."

"Tincan Tomsen has gotten us tickets to attend his closing remarks. The only thing Tincan asks of us is that we do not disturb the proceedings if we attend. I don't think it's fair to say that we are honoring Topp in any way, but Tincan stuck his neck out for us and we don't want to embarrass him or the Naval Institute. I will be at your side, and I think Tincan will be there; can you promise to sit quietly and just hear whatever it is he has to say? Admiral Tomsen said he'll be sure that we're in the back of the hall."

Becky absorbed everything Tom told her and sat quietly for a long moment. Finally, she replied. "Talking about this with my mom was actually easier than I had expected. I know that when she came out of the hospital, she was in much better control of her emotions than she had been, and certainly more in control then she was when she had the breakdown. She even was able to read and comment upon all of the two dozen or so newspaper clippings that Dr. Annie gathered for us. We cried together a lot, and she brought out an album of photographs that I had never seen. She was younger then and beautiful, and dad was tall and handsome. Do you remember my telling you how much I enjoyed carousels and merry-go-rounds? There was one picture where they were standing together on the merry-go-round at Hershey Park. You could tell how much they were in love. Perhaps that love was passed down to me, I don't know. If we go to Annapolis, Tom, I make a solemn promise to you that I will not embarrass you, nor Admiral Tomsen nor the United States Navy."

CHAPTER 14
DER ALTE HERR

Thursday, August 22, 1968 – Annapolis Md.

On August 22nd, they arrived at the Naval Institute, invitations in hand, and walked to the conference at the former Naval Hospital, near gate eight of the Naval Academy. Admiral Tomsen met them and escorted them into the auditorium.

Seated toward the back of the room they listened to the moderator's introduction:

Rear Admiral Erich Topp was the third most successful German U-Boot commander of World War II, for which he was awarded the Ritterkreuz des Eisernen Kreuzes mit Eichenlaub und Schwertern (the Knight's Cross of the Iron Cross with Oak Leaves and Swords). During the war, he was responsible for the loss of some 35 ships totaling 197,460 gross register tons (GRT).

As captain of the Type VII submarine, U-552, he participated in attacks on convoy HX-156 on 31 October 1941, which resulted in the loss of the destroyer USS Reuben James (DD-245), the first US warship to be sunk in World War II. After many subsequent postings, he took command of U-2513, aboard which he surrendered in May 1945 at Horten, Norway, where he was interned.

*Returning to Germany to complete his university education, he gradu-
ated from the Technical University of Hanover in 1950 with a degree
in engineering. He worked as an architect for the next eight years.*

*Shortly after the establishment of the FRG, he was commissioned
into the Bundesmarine in 1958, and was posted as Chief of Staff
at NATO's Military Committee in Washington. In 1963, he was
appointed Chief of Staff in command of the fleet, and in 1965, he
was simultaneously appointed chief of the operations staff of the Navy
and Deputy Chief of the Navy of the Federal Republic. He was pro-
moted to Rear Admiral in 1966, as a tribute to his efforts in rebuild-
ing the navy and the establishment of the transatlantic alliance.
Konteradmiral Topp: Ein herzliches Dankeschön und Willkommen!*

Rear Admiral Topp, in his dress blue uniform, rose and walked pur-
posefully to the lectern. "Thank you for that excellent introduction,
Captain," he said in nearly unaccented English. "For nearly 30 years I have
been honored to serve my country in two very different navies, and now in
the twilight of my career I welcome the opportunity to reflect on the lessons learned over a long, and sometimes very arduous career.

I would like to begin my otherwise chronological narrative with a wartime experience that placed me in a politically borderline situation and that
has determined how I look back on my life from a moral perspective. An
excerpt from the war diaries of the U-boat high command:"

*In the morning hours of October 31, 1941, U-552 sighted the British
convoy HX156 in the central Atlantic. Its screen consisted of five destroyers. At 0834 the commanding officer, Kapitänleutnant Topp sank one
of the escorts, USS Reuben James, in position latitude 51' 59" North, 27'
05" West. The US destroyer belonged to the escort of the British convoy
even before the United States entered the war or on December 11, 1941.*

"Adolph Hitler had hinted at his expansionist intentions as early as in *Mein Kampf.* Later, in 1937, he provided details about his designs. This does not mean that Hitler acted according to a carefully prepared plan. His determination to expand Germany's borders, however, made war inevitable. The war was prepared and carried out in such a way that it took a coalition of world powers six years to bring Germany down militarily.

After the Blitzkrieg against Poland and the West, Hitler's territorial acquisitions remained unrecognized under international law. For this reason Hitler felt driven to keep up the momentum of conquest, to add expansion to expansion, just as others had done before him: Alexander the Great, Julius Caesar, and Napoleon. In addition there was a racial hubris and the notion of a "people without space." I compare Hitler to Alexander, Caesar, Napoleon and other empire builders, only in terms of their determination conquest of territory, certainly not with regard to their overall personality or historical status.

Historians disagree whether a politically consolidated continental Europe, based on a generous peace with France and a confederation of states, would have been feasible. Some, like Joachim Fest, point out that England, backed by the United States, would not have accepted such a concept of Europe.

In reality, Hitler did not achieve any such political solutions. Prodded on by the Allied demand for unconditional surrender, he felt compelled to extend his expansionist drive. This was a strategic mistake, considering the fatal gulf between Germany's means and objectives. Hitler's dilemma was rendered worse by countless political miscalculations and senseless crimes, not to mention his pathological determination to carry on, regardless of consequence. In the Napoleonic era world power status hinged on hegemony over the continent, including Russia, and on defeat of England. By the 20th century it also meant the destruction of American power.

For a while, Hitler was careful enough not to provoke the United States. To the contrary, he deliberately put up with provocations from the other side, as these examples bear out:

- September 1940: Delivery of 50 destroyers to England.

- March, 1941: Lend Lease Act, enabling England to buy US materials without paying cash

- April 1941: Extension of the already unusual 300-mile-wide "Pan American security zone" (to 30 degrees W longitude)'. Inside this zone US forces shadowed and reported German ships until they could be seized by the British. This behavior was difficult to reconcile with a policy of neutrality.

- Since April 1941: US forces escort British convoys in the Western Hemisphere.

- April 10, 1941: The US destroyer *Niblack* attacks a German U-boat.

- July 7, 1941: US forces occupy Iceland as a military base.

- September 4, 1941: A British aircraft sights a German U-boat, drops depth charges, and reports its position to the USS destroyer *Greer*; the latter pursues the U-boat. The submarine in turn fires two torpedoes against the *Greer* under the assumption that she is a British warship. The *Greer* responds with 11 depth charges.

Even though the US president was informed that the German U-boat did not know the destroyer's nationality, Navy Secretary Frank Knox used all available means to seize and destroy German surface and underwater "Pirates."

Compared to President Roosevelt's "short of war" policy, the German naval high command exercised extreme restraint in its actions toward the United States.

Then, in the dawn hours of October 31, 1941, I attacked and sank an escort vessel out of a British convoy. A short while later we learned by monitoring radio broadcasts that the destroyer belonged to a country with which we were not at war: the *Reuben James* of the United States.

I immediately remembered Germany's resumption of unrestricted submarine warfare as the occasion of the US entry into World War I and was thus aware how politically explosive the sinking of the destroyer might become. Until we reached base, I was alone with my thoughts. As far as international law was concerned, I felt no qualms whatsoever. After all, I have attacked a British convoy being escorted by warships. Nevertheless, I felt alone. The tension a man endures when he thinks he is making history, however unintentional, is indeed enormous.

Only much later did I learn that the political course had already been laid out, and that history would merely shrug its shoulders over an incident such as the sinking of the *Reuben James*. Of course, I was ordered to Paris where I had to describe in every detail the attack and the sinking to Admiral Karl Donitz of the U-boat high command.

I also began to realize that Germany's declaration of war against the United States after Japan's action of December 7, 1941, was not merely the result of the rational expectations one encounters in the course of all great territorial expansions, and but that political forces were likewise at work. To this one must add the underestimation of US resources in terms of manpower and economic potential. I can still hear today the snide comments Hitler made in his table talks at his headquarters. He made fun, for example, of Roosevelt's physical paralysis and of the "Liberty" and

"Victory" ships being allegedly so poorly designed that they could not withstand Atlantic storms.

From time to time, moral arguments have entered the debate over the origin of Hitler's hubris. His racial manias and their consequences, and his genocide of the Jews, and the enslavement of the Slavic peoples are said to have pushed the world into a total war against Germany. However terrible and incomprehensible this genocide based on racism will remain, one must understand that it was not the moral reason behind the US entry into the war on the Allied side. Today, we know that neither the Americans nor the British helped the Jews when it would have been possible; indeed, they refused to do so in specific cases. In the end it was Germany's, and also Japan's, territorial aspirations and the Allied refusal to give in to such expansionist drives that made the war both total and global.

The political dimensions of the sinking of the *Reuben James* is not without ambivalence. The US media used the incident deliberately to incite the public mood in favor of entering the war against Germany. They did so, not by analyzing the legitimacy of the attack under international law following a political and military provocation on part of the United States, but by emphasizing the national challenge posed by those "Hitler Pirates."

Even Woody Guthrie, as early as November 1941, wrote a song about the sinking of the *Reuben James* that was sung everywhere: *"Did you have a friend on the good Reuben James?"* According to the second and third verses, the destroyer *"watched for the U-boats, and waited for the fight,"* and *"now our mighty battleships will steam the mighty main."* I will not equate poetical license with political will, but it seems easy to prove that, already in this critical phase of the war, the media and the politicians worked closely together on all sides.

126

On November 14, just two weeks after the *Reuben James* had gone down as the first US warship lost in World War II, Roosevelt asked Congress to pass legislation that would allow the arming of US merchant vessels. Reflecting the country's mood, Congress agreed to the request by a vote of 212 to 194. With this measure the neutrality acts began became history and the US entry into the war occurred *de facto*.

When Hitler declared war on the United States on December 11, 1941, four days after the Japanese raid against Pearl Harbor, he did so not as a result of American public opinion but under political pressure. I believe his need to expand his territorial conquests played a vital role.

What mattered for me was the nagging notion of being caught up in the making of world events and the need to work out what the sinking of the *Reuben James* meant in political terms. I had the feeling of being somewhat involved in weighty political decisions which, given the experience of World War I, seemed most ominous to me.

On that morning, the hit, as observed from the boat's conning tower in the dawn's gathering light, appeared to us as follows: "An explosion some 1000 yards away. The rear part of the ship sank first, its unsecured depth charges detonating in a huge secondary explosion and throwing tall columns of water skyward. A nearby destroyer picked up survivors. We left the scene."

This formative impression stood at the very beginning of my wartime experiences, and it changed my life. Since then, I've often had occasion to contemplate a famous quotation from Jacob Burchardt's reflections on history: "You cannot draw lessons from history for the next time around, but you can become wiser for all time." I have never attained this high level of insight. To the contrary, I have learned that the passing of decades does not cushion anything. As the years go by, they may blur the words of the past, but they cannot stop the onslaught of the images. These images continue to haunt me; they take away my sleep.

But this I <u>do know</u>, with absolutely moral certainty. **For over a year we had engaged destroyers of the same class and identical profile as that of the Reuben James.** *The ships, obsolete as they may have been, were an extreme danger to our submarines. One has only to compare the number of boats sunk before and after these destroyers arrived, crewed by British, Canadian, "Free French" and Norwegian crews, and flying the national ensigns of these countries. In the pre-dawn hours of October 31,1941, at periscope depth under blackout conditions and at great range, I defy <u>any</u> ship's officer to accurately identify the nationality of any such destroyer operating at flank speed and attempting to blind you with powerful spotlights, particularly one assumed to be neutral and concerning which, he has strict orders not to engage under any circumstances.*

The deaths of any seamen are tragic, but nevermore so than when a "non-combatant" takes advantage of the fog of war for nefarious purposes. What those purposes might have been, I leave to you historians to deduce and evaluate. Thank you, and after a short break shall be happy to attempt to answer such questions as you might have. [1].

Admiral Tomsen tapped Tom's knee, and they all rose and left the auditorium. "Discretion is the better part of valor," he whispered out of earshot of Becky. Call me when you get back up to Baltimore."

Rear Admiral Erich Topp shortly before his retirement from the German Navy

CHAPTER 15
MORE QUESTIONS THAN ANSWERS

Thursday, August 22, 1968 – Baltimore

When they reached the parking lot, Becky confronted Tom. "What was that all about? Your friend Admiral Tomsen hustled us out of there as if the hall was on fire. I promised you I would not embarrass you or the Navy, and I wouldn't. I'm angry that you didn't trust me."

"I'm sorry, Becky. He surprised me, too. I've known Tincan for a long time; he never was one to take unnecessary risks. That said, what did you think about Admiral Topp's address?"

Well, as far as I know he's the first Nazi I ever met. And everything he said seem to be self-justification. While he was up there, pontificating, it occurred to me that he's probably just as old as my dad would have been, had he not been torpedoed by Admiral Topp's U-boat. I hope you're not planning to invite him to dinner."

Tom drove silently up the Governor Ritchie Highway toward Baltimore. After several minutes, he replied. "May I tell you a true story, Becky?"

"Don't tell me that you understand, because I know that you don't."

"It's not about that. It's a true story, and I know it's true because it happened to me." Becky did not reply, and Tom began.

"Oh, it was about eight or nine years ago, now. As a matter of fact, I had just become master of the *Rita E*. We pulled into Hamburg, and figured to be there for a couple days. It was midsummer and the weather was delightful. Rather than hang around the ship with nothing much to do, I asked our first mate to look after things for a while. I went into Hamburg, found the railway station on the Bahnhoffstrasse and purchased a ticket on the hourly train to Kiel. I had known from my readings and from my experience during the war that Kiel had been an important base for U-boats. The journey took about an hour and, when I arrived in Kiel I rode a tram about six miles north to the town of Laboe. Quite close to the last tram stop, I could see a large monument in the distance. It was a memorial to the thirty thousand German seamen and officers who died on the U-boats in World War II. Nearly three out of four submariners were lost at sea, Becky. It was quite a large and impressive monument, about 280 feet tall, and at the base on thick concrete pillars was a type VII submarine, the U995."

"I sat on a bollard and tried to get in touch with my feelings. I'm not very keen on churches or cathedrals, but there was a – how do I describe it? – a *spiritual* quality surrounding that place. And as I sat there, surrounded by the hustle and bustle and smells of a working dockyard, I thought of all the men who died on the three U-boats which I and my crew had sunk in the North Atlantic. I never met any of them; I didn't even know the number or names of their boats. They may have been fanatical Nazis; they may just have been innocent young farm kids caught up in a war started by a madman, for all I know."

"But this I do know, Becky. Most of them, I suspect, were also just about my age; and I'm here and they are not. They were, after all, 'the enemy', at least that's what we were told. And I suppose, that's what their leaders told them about us. But if I have learned anything wandering around the world, it's that today's enemy may well be tomorrow's friend. Admiral Topp was my enemy. I would have gladly depth-charged him into oblivion had I had the chance. And today he is our ally. I don't know..."

"Why were we there in the North Atlantic, Tom? All of this happened to my dad before war was ever declared. What business did we have escorting someone else's ships to someone else's country? I've always taken solace in the thought that my father died defending our country. What did Britain or Iceland mean to us that caused a good man to die a frightful death? Tell me that, Captain, if you can."

He sat silently again, concentrating on the traffic as they approached Baltimore. "I can't, Becky. That's a question for historians, philosophers or theologians. God help us if we leave that question to generals or admirals. Or even worse, God forbid that we leave those decisions in the hands of politicians."

"Let's skip going out to dinner tonight, Tom, if that's okay with you. I'm not really up to it. I saw you have a stockpile of TV dinners in your freezer compartment. Let's eat-in tonight, okay?"

Tom nodded.

"You'll have to put your life in my hands tonight, Tom. Even TV dinners stretch my culinary skills. But let's stop off and buy a bottle of wine to go with the meal. What wine is recommended as the perfect complement for TV dinners?"

"I don't know, but I suspect it's nothing with a cork in the bottle. Screw tops seem more appropriate in this instance, don't you think?"

They stopped at the "Twenty-First Amendment Liquor Store" on Route 40, and Becky returned with a bottle of Boone's Farm in one hand and a Bottle of Abie's Irish Rose in the other. "These are Vintage-Tuesday, according to the clerk. He said they taste better if you surround them with a paper bag but I bet they'll go very well with tonight's dinner."

The wine did go surprisingly well with the Swanson's Hungry Man dinners of Salisbury steak, mashed potatoes and some unidentified green vegetables. "All we need are a couple of TV tables and we could watch Bonanza just like we do at home," Becky remarked.

"I've had worse meals aboard ship," Tom replied. "Although I can't remember when."

They decided to make an early night of it, and retired early. But both spent a great deal of the night thinking of what they had heard during the day.

After breakfast the next morning, Tom helped Becky clear the kitchen table and then retrieved an inlaid mahogany chest from his closet. Highly polished, it was clear that it protected something of great value. Tom opened the chest and showed Becky the antique Carl Plaith sextant he'd used since his days at the Maine Maritime Academy. "This was a gift from my father, and dates back to the days when *his* father sailed as master of coastal packets out of Camden, Maine. Encased in a small gold frame inside the red-velvet lined chest was a small card, inscribed in elegant Gothic script: *'Karl Plath, Instrumentalist, Stubbenhuk 25, Nähe des Kanal Herrerngraben, Hamburg"*.

"Oh, Tom. That is really an exquisite instrument. But tell me, are you afraid the condo has sailed away during the night?" She peered dramatically out the kitchen window.

"No, not at all," Tom laughed. "But look here. In these small drawers I store my navigation instruments." He removed a set of parallel rulers, dividers, and a compass rose from the neat little compartments underneath the sextant.

Tom took the maps and charts which he had purchased in Newfoundland and spread them across the table. "I just want to get a better mental picture as to what happened that morning, and the best way for me to do that is bending over a chart table. And since I don't have a chart table handy, the kitchen table will have to do. Here, help me out. Grab some small cans from the pantry and put one on each corner of this chart. We'll make a mariner of you yet, Becky!"

Once the chart was securely in place, Tom retrieved his copy of the escort patrol report. "The *Reuben James* was torpedoed here, at 51°59'N 27°05' W." Tom quickly used his instruments to plot that position with a small x on one of the larger scale charts. "We know the weather conditions were clear, and it was approaching dawn. We also know the direction of travel of the convoy, and that *Reuben James* was on the flank. That would make the U-552 somewhat north of the convoy track, and the *Reuben James* would have been slightly to his starboard and about a mile and a half away."

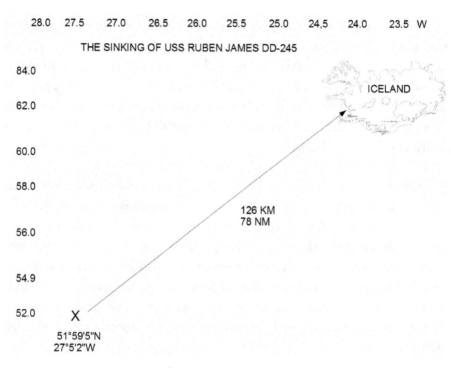

28.0   27.5   27.0   26.5   26.0   25.5   25.0   24,5   24.0   23.5 W

THE SINKING OF USS RUBEN JAMES DD-245

84.0

                                                                    ICELAND
62.0

60.0

58.0

                                        126 KM
                                        78 NM
56.0

54.9

52.0   X
       51°59'5"N
       27°5'2"W

Tom's Kitchen Table Plot

"Where can we get more information, Tom? I mean, somewhere there has to be a record of sunrise and sunset times and all that stuff going back to 1941, doesn't there?"

"There certainly is, Becky, and we can find out that information in any Nautical Almanac. But what I think we ought to do is to sit down with a notepad and list all of the things that are bothering us about this. I, for one, have lots of questions floating around in my mind."

Becky took down a magnetized notepad from the front of the refrigerator. "It's not very big Tom, but I think it will do."

"Okay, you can use a couple of pages if you need to. I'll think out loud and you just write down what I say. We can do this like a stream of consciousness."

Tom began:

1. What exactly did the Destroyers for Bases agreement entail?

2. What classes of destroyers were traded to the British and the Canadians?

3. How many ships were involved? When did it happen?

4. Reuben James was a Clemson class destroyer. How many Clemson's or similar destroyers were involved in the neutrality patrol in October, 1941?

5. Did FDR, the Secretary of the Navy, or the Chief of Naval Operations know that the Reuben James risked being misidentified as a British or Canadian warship?

If they didn't know, what were they expecting? And how did the incident with the USS Greer two weeks beforehand play into all of this?

"Get all of that?" Tom asked.

"Yes, I think so. Does this mean we're going back to the Naval Historical Center again?"

"No, Becky, I don't think that's such a good idea. For one thing, we've taken up a lot of their time already. For another, I'm not sure that I would completely trust any information coming from Navy sources on questions such as these. We are in luck, though. While you were back in Pennsylvania and I had just returned from Newfoundland, I spent a morning wandering around the history and technology sections of the Enoch Pratt Central Library, on Cathedral Street in downtown Baltimore. The place is huge, Becky. In addition to serving as the main library for the City and County of Baltimore, it's the site of the state library as well. When I was there, I chanced to meet one of their researchers, and I asked him if he would help us find what we're looking for. If you want to head over there today, let's get cleaned up and we can get down there within a half hour or so."

Becky suggested that it might be best if they called ahead to determine if the librarian had any additional information for them. Tom agreed and retrieved a business card from his wallet. He dialed the library and asked for Mr. Alfred Daley. When Mr. Daley came on line, he remembered Tom, and told him he had uncovered addition information which might meet his needs. They agreed to meet shortly after lunch.

CHAPTER 16
ROOT CAUSES

Friday, August 23, 1968 – Baltimore

When Tom and Becky arrived on the spacious second-floor of the Pratt Library, Mr. Daley was waiting for them. The tall, well-dressed and well-spoken African-American asked a fellow librarian to cover the front desk, and suggested that they adjourn to a nearby table in the corner of the reading room. The windows were open and there was a pleasant breeze cooling the area. "This is my favorite table in the entire library," he said.

Tom introduced Becky to Mr. Daley. She immediately was attracted to his deep but mellow baritone voice, and his slow and meticulous manner of speech. Clearly the middle-aged, articulate gentleman loved his job, and she looked forward to hearing the information that he had discovered for them.

"Before we start, Captain Tom and Miss Franks, I should tell you that I too have a keen personal interest in what happened in those pre-war days in the North Atlantic. I enlisted in the United States Coast Guard in 1938, and served for over 25 years. Now, in those days, we colored fellows could only serve as mess attendants, of course. I served both at sea and ashore as an officer's steward until 1948, when Mr. Truman integrated the military. I cross-rated, and finally retired as a Chief Yeoman in 1963. As fate would have it, I was aboard the cutter *USCGC Taney* (WPG-37) from 1941 through '43, attached to the North Atlantic neutrality patrol. We operated between Halifax and Hvalfjordur, Iceland for years. You probably recall that particularly desolate piece of real estate, captain. We Coasties called it 'Valley Forge,' partly because no one could pronounce the name in Icelandic, and partly, I suspect, because it brought to mind George Washington and the frozen encampments of 1777-78. Those were exciting days, indeed. We used to say that the Navy drilled to prepare for danger, but we Coasties lived it every day. Our unofficial motto was 'You have to go out, but you don't have to come back.'

"Perhaps the easiest way to help you understand all of this is to allow me to recite the story, based upon these documents that I have here. As you know, the Enoch Pratt library is also the official state library for Maryland, and we have inter-library loan arrangements throughout the state. Most of the documents we will be using today are on loan from the library at the Naval Academy at Annapolis, although some come from the Coast Guard base over at Curtis Bay. Everything is unclassified, and when we're finished here you are free to make copies for your own use, although, unfortunately, it will cost you a dime per page. Sadly, libraries are not a great priority for the taxpayers of Baltimore these days."

"Just like at home, sir." Becky interjected.

"Then let us begin. You asked for the history of the Destroyers for Bases agreement of 1940. By that point, the British had been at war with Germany for over a year, and things were not going well at all. They had lost a number of ships at the time of the Dunkirk evacuation, and were losing vital war materials through the sinking of cargo ships en route to the home islands. Mr. Churchill has said that this was the only time when he thought that the successful outcome of the war was in doubt. He implored Mr. Roosevelt to provide him the war materials to allow him to defeat the Axis. 'Give us the tools' he said, 'and we will finish the job!'

Mr. Roosevelt was amenable, but Congress certainly was not. On four separate occasions since 1939, Congress had voted for non-intervention.

140

Mr. Roosevelt however, had other ideas. His legal advisers told him that, so long as no cash payments were involved, he could negotiate a bartered agreement with Mr. Churchill. This he did, swapping 50 destroyers from the mothball fleet along the James River for military bases on British possessions in the Atlantic and Caribbean. Most historians now conclude that the United States got the better part of the deal, but Mr. Churchill was in no position to dicker. The destroyers were turned over to the British and Canadians in Halifax late in 1940."

"Captain Tom, I know that you are a military veteran and so you understand about the classifications of ships. The fifty destroyers were almost evenly divided among Clemson and Wickes classes, with a couple old Caldwells tossed in for good measure. All of these were flush-deck destroyers, with four tall funnels, although these were quickly reduced in size to decrease the silhouette and to improve stability in poor weather. The British and Canadians renamed these destroyers for towns or cities which were common to the USA and Great Britain or rivers that were common to the USA and Canada. After a short transition they began to escort convoys across the Atlantic."

"Shortly thereafter, Mr. Roosevelt unilaterally extended the 'Atlantic Sea Frontier' to 26 degrees west longitude, roughly south of Iceland. The United States assumed responsibility for convoy escorts from Newfoundland to Iceland in the early autumn of 1941. The vast majority of US ships on escort duty were much newer destroyers, generally of the Gleeves and Benson classes. But a total of 10 Clemson class destroyers were also assigned. One of those, of course, was *Reuben James*.

"I served on two Gleeves class destroyers myself," remarked Tom,"the *Hanlon* and the *Dennis N. Terry*. They were excellent ships."

"They were indeed. But consider this. There were 50 flush deck four-stack destroyers operating under British and Canadian flags. There were only 10 operating under the Stars and Stripes. It was at this time, too, that the Coast Guard was placed, kicking and screaming, under Navy control, a situation which none of us in the Coast Guard particularly appreciated. But no matter, that's what we did.

I checked the records at the Naval Academy, and during the last three weeks of October 1941, only three Clemson class destroyers were active. One of those was the *USS Greer*, which two weeks before had been involved in an incident in which a German U-boat attacked it under highly suspicious circumstances. Fortunately, the torpedo missed, but Greer was being repaired at St. John's at the time. The other two were *USS Tarbell* and the *USS Reuben James*, on opposite flanks of convoy HX-156. All three had been operating extensively in the waters west of Iceland. The autumn weather in the North Atlantic is never good; it's cold, foggy, and the seas are usually very rough. President Roosevelt knew that; he had been secretary of the Navy at the end of World War I. Navy Secretary Frank Knox knew that; his father was from Nova Scotia and his mother from Prince Edward Island, and he had sailed those waters himself many times. The Chief of Naval Operations, Admiral Stark knew that; he had completed an around the world cruise with the Atlantic Fleet earlier in his career. And most certainly, Admiral Ernest King knew that better than anyone. He was Commander in Chief, Atlantic Fleet, during the period. He had argued against providing the ships to the British, and it required direct orders in the name of the president for him to prepare the ships and to deliver them at Halifax. He also was ordered to allow US forces to work jointly as escorts with Allied warships. And all knew that under wartime conditions the probability of mistaken identification would be very high."

"And so we come to the key question. To what advantage did our ships operate as escorts for British convoys in the North Atlantic? With 50 additional destroyers, and crash programs in British and Canadian dockyards turning out Frigates and Corvettes faster than it ever been done before, did the British really need our support? Destroyers of these types were not particularly well-suited to serve as convoy escorts, in any event. Using thirty-knot destroyers to herd eight-knot convoys was akin to employing greyhounds to herd sheep and goats, according to one Royal Navy Commodore. We were not escorting convoys all the way to Britain either; they detoured to Hvalfjordur and picked up British escorts for the eastern part of the routes. The diversion was solely to contain the US ships within the artificial continental boundary set by President Roosevelt. A boundary, by the way, that was neither recognized by nor had any impact upon the movements of German U-boats. So why were *Reuben James* and the others sent into harm's way?"

"And how many U.S. flagged ships were in convoy HX-156, Mr. Daley?"

"None, Becky. Zero. Zilch. There were 23 British, 10 Norwegian, 4 Dutch, 4 from Panama, 2 from Belgium and a Pole. And consider this, Miss Franks. Recently two French journalists published a block-buster paper disclosing that the British had been decoding German U-boat radio signals at Bletchley Park, Buckinghamshire, since mid-1940. They called the system *Enigma*, and distribution was limited to a very small number of senior officials. In August 1941 however, when Mr. Churchill visited Mr. Roosevelt and announced the Atlantic Charter, he informed the president of this development, and they agreed to share information about the locations of U-boats in the North Atlantic. The British referred to anyone who had access to the decrypted messages as *Bigots,* and Mr. Roosevelt is known to have shared this information with both the Secretary of the Navy and the Chief of Naval Operations. For all intents and purposes, we can consider that the United States Navy knew the approximate location of the U-552 from the time she left the coast of Brittany until the time she returned."

"Now consider the disposition of the escort vessels accompanying convoy HX-156. The *Reuben James* and the *USS Tarbell* were on opposite flanks of the convoy, in the positions that merchant mariners called the 'coffin corners.' Giving the heading of the convoy, a U-boat could either be on its starboard or port flank, and still have a clear shot at the closest escort. And with the prevailing conditions, it's not unbelievable that a U-boat skipper would think that he's firing at a Canadian or a British warship. Personally,

I believe this is the most likely scenario to explain the otherwise inexplicable decision of the U-boat captain to blatantly disregard Hitler's direct orders not to engage the Americans under any circumstances."

"Now, Mr. Roosevelt was a complex man. He often said that he chose not to let his left-hand know what his right-hand was doing. He also believed strongly in the inevitability of war with Germany, perhaps more so than the likelihood of war with Japan. But there was a great isolationist feeling in the country at that time. Charles Lindbergh, the German American Bund and half of Congress were adamantly opposed to becoming involved in yet another European war. Was he looking for an excuse? Did we place those few American destroyers in harm's way as 'bait'? We may never know. After all, it's not the sort of thing that would ever be recorded or written down. But I think standards of jurisprudence which apply in every court ought apply. Did he know, or *should* he have known, and did he act with willful aforethought, so that by his actions he placed the lives of hundreds of men at risk? At risk, not from death from an enemy with whom we were at war, but death through involvement in the wars of other nations. It is a sobering, and disturbing thought."

Becky sat quietly and listened, tears streaming down her cheeks.

"I have a great deal of supporting documentation here for you, everything from the climatic conditions on October 31, 1941, to lists of the various ships involved in the Destroyers for Bases agreement, to a list of the dispositions of the Clemson class destroyers during the same period. You may have these to do with them what you will."

Tom and Becky sat in stunned silence. All of a sudden, all of the small details which they'd learned from patrol reports from the US escort and the desk logs and statements of the skipper of U-552 fell into place. "*Bait*, Mr. Daley, is that what you would call it? Did my father and his shipmates die just to give President Roosevelt an excuse to enter the war? Because if he did, then they died in vain. The sinking of *Reuben James* did nothing, absolutely nothing, to change the course of events. We were at war with both Germany and Japan six weeks later."

Alfred Daley replied, sadly. "I'm certain that no one will ever prove or disprove this. One of the challenges of history is that it is open to many interpretations. I know this personally: For the past ten years or so I have been researching the history of my own family, the stories of my ancestors not only here but in Africa. What is true, what is legend? All is open to interpretation. In this case, I don't think there's a smoking gun; there are just 115 dead men lying at the bottom of the North Atlantic."

Tom and Becky thanked Mr. Daley for his contribution to understanding what had happened, and wished him well with his personal research. "What a wonderful man, he is," she told Tom as they returned to the car. "I certainly hope that he finds his family's roots. But I think, at long last, we've reached the end of the road. The quest may never be complete, but at least I feel satisfied that I know what happened, and now perhaps I understand why. I'll grab the train tomorrow morning; I have a new semester on the horizon. But you and your friends have been so very kind and generous to me, and I'll always be grateful to you. I do have one more thing to tell you though, and it's been bothering me for a while."

"And what's that, Becky?"

"I not only participated, but helped plan the protest match in Philadelphia, Tom. You've been so kind to me that I thought you should know 'the rest of the story,' as that fellow says on the radio."

"Don't give it a second thought, kiddo. You were only doing what you thought right."

"Thanks, Tom. And good luck to you in your search, too."

USS Reuben James (DD245) in action in the N. Atlantic, October 1941

HMS Broadway, Clemson Class Destroyer

HMS Charlestown, Clemson Class Destroyer

HMCS St.Croix, Clemson Class Destroyer

CHAPTER 17
ASK THE CHIEF

Wednesday, August 28, 1968 – Washington

Tom returned to the condo and spent the next several days occupied with minor housekeeping issues which needed to be completed during his limited time ashore. He found a dentist who was willing to take a walk-in patient, spent an afternoon at Hecht's department store and attended a doubleheader at Memorial Stadium as the Orioles beat the Yankees by scores of 3-2, and 2-1. He also enjoyed several mornings at various bookstores around the city, replenishing his supply of paperbacks for the long voyages ahead.

Late one Tuesday morning, he received a phone call from Tincan Tomsen. "Admiral Moore and his team have returned from Vietnam. I got a call yesterday afternoon from MCPON (Master Chief Petty Officer of the Navy) Del White; both he and Sergeant Major Herb Sauer uncovered some information to share with you. I have no idea what they found, nor how significant it might be in understanding the circumstances of Mary Kay's death, but both he and Sauer are willing to meet with you on Friday, and he suggests meeting at the Marine Corps Barracks at Eighth and I Streets in Washington. Sergeant Major Sauer keeps a secondary office there, so there's plenty of privacy. I'll come over with you, if you like."

"There is no need for that, Tincan. I think I can find the barracks without too much trouble.""I'd really like to come along, Tom. You've got me interested in all of this, especially after our run-in with Florence Nightingale's chief bedpan assistant, the Wicked Witch of the West. I'll come along for moral support. How does 11 AM sound to you? That will give Sauer some time to get up from Quantico."

"Once again, Tincan, you've turned out to be a real shipmate. I'll see you at 11."

Friday dawned, cloudy and cooler than it had been earlier in the week. Tom left early, and arrived at the Marine barracks shortly after 10:30. He waited in the parking lot until he saw Admiral Tomsen arrive, and they entered together. The gate guard gave them directions to the Sergeant Major's suite.

The young lance corporal in Sergeant Major Sauer's office greeted them cordially. "The Master Chief Petty Officer of the Navy has just arrived and he's in with the Sergeant Major now. I'll just run in there and tell them that you have arrived."

In a few minutes, they were sitting in the formally decorated office of the Sergeant Major of the Marine Corps. Both Sergeant Major Sauer and Master Chief White were grizzled veterans of the Second World War. "I wonder what those guys look like in their dress blue uniforms," Tom thought to himself. "Both have chevrons that go all the way up their sleeves, and I suspect that the rows of ribbons on their dress uniforms reach up to the shoulder and may even flip over and start coming down the back. Officers run the Navy, but chiefs run the ships. And I bet it's the same among our Jarhead friends."

After the customary coffee prepared by the lance corporal, they got down to business. Master Chief White began the briefing.

150

"Admiral Moore described your situation, Captain," he said, using Tom's formal title. "First of all, sir, you have my condolences and I'm sure you have Herb's as well.

Sergeant Major Sauer nodded in agreement.

"In order to optimize the short amount of time we had in the Danang area, Sergeant Major and I decided to split up and to investigate this as thoroughly as we could, given our limitations. Admiral Moore was scheduled to go out to the *USS Sanctuary* to award purple hearts to wounded Navy and Marine personnel; I went along with him and, while he was having lunch in the Wardroom there, I conversed with Master Chief Hospital Corpsman Drake, the senior enlisted man on board. He didn't know Mary Kay, but he knew staff who had been there during late 1966, and he introduced me to them. One nurse in particular was very helpful. She had been a classmate of Mary Kay's during Nurse Corps orientation, and they became friends again when Mary Kay reported aboard *Sanctuary*. She told me that Mary Kay was an excellent nurse and a great shipmate. She was particularly interested in pediatric nursing. Now, that's a field that has limited opportunity in the Navy, of course, but she had worked in the pediatric clinics at Naval Hospital Staten Island before reporting on board. She also said that the senior nurse on their ward 'took Mary Kay under her wing' and looked out for her, if for no other reason than this was her first sea duty. She also mentioned, and I say this with some sensitivity, that Mary Kay and the senior nurse had '*become very close.*' That's her emphasis, not mine. In any event, when the opportunity arose for a 30-day TAD [Temporary Assignment to Duty] ashore, she pushed Mary Kay to apply and, so this young nurse said, 'made it happen.' She knew that MEDCAPs usually spent a great deal of time working with kids, and thought that it would be something that your daughter would enjoy."

"A couple of weeks into the TAD, the nursing staff were told that, because of the life-threatening injuries you suffered while at sea, Mary Kay received an emergency leave to return to the States. She never returned to the *USS Sanctuary*, and no one knew how to contact her. And that's the latest information they had."

"I never was injured at sea," Tom exclaimed. "That's total bullshit!"

"So I've learned," Master Chief White replied. "Maybe this is a good point to turn things over to Sergeant Major Sauer. His inquiries were somewhat more fruitful than mine."

Sauer began: "This is going to be a difficult story to recount, Captain. I wish that I did not have to tell you these things. I've been in the Marine Corps since 1938, and I've had to deliver an awful lot of bad news to the parents and loved ones of my Marines. And it never gets any easier."

"Your daughter was indeed assigned to a MEDCAP, working in an area between Danang and the Hi-Van pass along highway QN-1. And there was, in fact, a large Catholic orphanage in the area. Because the area was not secure at night, the MEDCAP team billeted at a Seabee camp at Red Beach, about six clicks north of Danang city. For security purposes, the female members of the team returned to the city each night and billeted at camp Tien Sha, the headquarters of Naval Support Activity, Danang. For some reason, your daughter stopped off at the White Elephant facility downtown, alongside the Han River. The White Elephant building, at 54 Bach Dang Street, housed the administrative offices of the Naval Support Activities in a former hotel and adjacent warehouses. There can be any number of reasons why she did so: Personnel records, the communications center and a host of other organizations are located there. I contacted an old friend, Master Sergeant Zadruga of the First Marine Division at Hill 327, which was the closest major Marine Corps unit in the area. He helped me identify the Korean contractor who drove the bus between the MEDCAP site at Nam O and the city. He vaguely recalls dropping one female officer at White Elephant, and returning the rest to Tien Sha."

"Master Sergeant Zadruga and I then spoke at length with the officer in charge at White Elephant, a Navy commander by the name of Morris. While he was not in country in '66, he allowed us to interview a Mr. Nguyen, who had been the night barman in the small officer's club there for several years. He remembers that night vividly, based, I suppose, on what happened afterwards. He recalled that a woman, dressed in fatigues, came into the club sometime around 1930 local time. He mentioned that the chow hall closed at 1800 hours and that the club served sandwiches and other 'pub grub' as a service to stragglers. He saw the woman take her food – he doesn't recall exactly what – and sit at a table in the rear of the room. He also saw three civilians (Master Sergeant Zadruga believes strongly that they may have been contractors for Air America), come in and sit near her."

Tincan Tomsen intervened. "Do you know anything about Air America, Tom?" he asked.

"No, I know American Airlines, but I can't imagine what they would be doing there."

"They are as different as night and day," Tincan responded. "Air America is the CIA's own private little airline. They do all kinds of things, none of which even remotely resemble American Airlines. Their pilots are basically cowboys; they fly into all kinds of remote landing strips, and do all sorts of things, many of which are so highly classified that we common-ers may never know what they're all about."

The Sergeant Major continued. "Master Sergeant Zadruga reminded me that the position of American civilians in Vietnam is difficult to describe. The one thing he told me, and I remember this from my own tour there in '65, is that the civilians have little respect for the military, and the military have even less respect for the civilians."

"He also pointed out that one entire wing of the White Elephant building was given over to Air America, ostensibly as a warehouse. However, those familiar with the building told us that it also serves as a billet and general hangout for Air America crews when they were on the deck in Danang. That wing is super-secure; no outsiders can get in there. There are no windows, the walls are thick, and doors are secured by cipher locks. And, our Marines tell us, these are not the kind of cipher locks you could pick up in a hardware store at home; these are very high security. And I suppose that is understandable, given the nature of the CIA/Air America's work in Vietnam. Zadruga, who is on his second tour in-country, has heard rumors that as far as the Viet Cong are concerned, the facility is like the Roach Motel: They check in, but they never check out."

"Did the bar manager remember who any of these fellows were?" asked Tom.

"He did, yes, at least in the case of one guy. His name is Gino Panderes, generally referred to as the 'Giant Panda', who was station manager for Danang. He was a big fat civilian, who I believe to be a retired Army major or lieutenant colonel. He was, by all accounts, a thoroughly vile human being. He was fond of Hawaiian shirts and cargo shorts, highlighted by a pearl-handled chromed 45-caliber pistol which he wore everywhere, including inside the White Elephant itself. To put this in perspective, the complex was about as dangerous as your average suburban mall at home, although Danang itself occasionally came under rocket and mortar attack, but usually on the outskirts. But it gives you an idea of what kind of person we're dealing with here."

"The barman recalled that all three of the Air America people seemed to be mildly intoxicated when they arrived. They were boisterous, but no more so than your average junior officer. At some point they joined the woman at her table and things appeared normal for a weekday evening in Danang. Sometime later the entire group got up and left the club. It's not at all clear that the woman left voluntarily; the barman was busy and did not see them depart."

"After interviewing the barman, Commander Morris introduced us to a number of Vietnamese who staffed the compound," Sergeant Major Sauer continued. "It's one of the sad facts of life in the American military these days that the only institutional memory resides with civilians, be they US or locals. In today's Armed Services climate, a generation is only about 18 months or less. In Vietnam, with our current rotation of individuals rather than integrated commands, there is nearly 100% turnover in 15 months, and we're looking back nearly two years now, remember."

"The good news is that the Vietnamese who work for us, or I should say *with* us, are generally loyal and conscientious. Master Sgt. Zadruga and I found several who were present the next morning, and who could recount what they observed. I must tell you, though, that we did promise them anonymity in return for their candor."

"What kind of work were these people doing?" Tom inquired.

"Well, unfortunately, most were menial employees. We spoke with several porters, cleaners, and one maintenance worker. We can summarize what they said fairly easily, because everyone we spoke to was consistent in their observations and recollections."

"Here's what we learned. Several of those interviewed had worked the mid-watch in various parts of the building. They heard what sounded like a confrontation; there was at least one female voice and possibly as many as three male voices. At least two of the cleaners recognized the voice of Panderes, the man they called the *'Map Dit Dien Cai Dau'(literally, 'Fattie sick head.)*' All of the male voices sounded intoxicated. The main door to the Air America wing makes a distinct sound when the cipher lock is opened or closed. Both of the cleaners recognized that sound; they heard it around 2200 or so. After the door closed, of course they could hear nothing. But later that evening, possibly around 2350 or so, they heard the door open and close again as if someone left the room and 15 minutes later they heard the door open again as if someone had returned. They thought nothing of this; it was in their eyes just usual activity on the part of the Americans."

"Go ahead, Herb, tell them what happened in the early morning hours of the 14th," interjected Master Chief White.

"Here's where things really get squirrely. A young Vietnamese by the name of Bach Le who did general maintenance for the compound arrived to begin his day shift around 0545. As was his custom, he started on the top floor of the main portion of the building and walked through each passageway in turn looking for burned out light bulbs, areas that needed special cleaning, and other maintenance-related issues. When he reached the first floor of the north wing, the Air America zone, he saw the door with the cipher lock standing ajar. This is something he had not seen before. He pushed open the door, and in the dim light could see a row of six small rooms, probably no larger than 12' x 12' each to his left. The door to the third room from the entrance was also ajar. Curious, but also fairly intrepid for a man in his position, he walked a few steps into the ware-house and peered through the door. He saw a naked Caucasian female, with blood covering her extremities and pooling on the bed sheets and on the floor beneath. He immediately ran to the front of the main building and summoned the Navy watch stander. It took only a few seconds for the watch stander to summons the JOOD and the Command Duty Officer, then he and the Vietnamese maintenance man returned to the Air America spaces and confirmed what the young man had seen. They immediately summoned a crew from the naval dispensary at Monkey Mountain, and phoned the Army Provost Marshal. MPs from the 101st Airborne, who had responsibility for the area, arrived within minutes as well. To their credit, none of the first individuals who discovered the scene disturbed it in any significant way. The Provost Marshals and the military police preserved the scene and took some Polaroid photographs, during which the medical crew arrived. There was a physician present and he pronounced the young woman as deceased at about 0645 that morning. At the direction of the Provost Marshal, an Army lieutenant colonel named Koslowski, the remains were removed to the forensic laboratory at camp Tien Sha. And that's where things become very difficult to comprehend."

"We did not have access, nor were we ever granted access, to any of the reports which emanated from this incident. I must tell you, Captain, as the Sergeant Major of the United States Marine Corps, I am not used to having my requests denied. I reported all of this to Admiral Moore, and he personally confronted the Commanding Officer of the Naval Support Activity, Danang. He was told, respectfully but decisively, that the U.S. Navy had no documentation whatsoever on file. The day after the body was removed to the forensic laboratory, several CIA representatives, accompanied by senior staff of Air America, flew up from Saigon and essentially took charge of the entire investigation.

"At this point, Captain," Master Chief White interjected, "both Sergeant Major Sauer and I determined that it was unlikely that we would discover any clear evidence which might be of use at a court martial or a civil proceeding. We've both been around the track many times, and one thing you learn at a racetrack is the smell of horseshit. And it was beginning to get very fragrant around Camp Tien Sha just about then."

Both Tom and Admiral Tomsen nodded. They too, understood.

"It's a stonewall, there is no other term to describe it," Sergeant Major Sauer interjected. "But, fortunately, right before we left Vietnam, the

Admiral's Flag Lieutenant received a telephone call from a Lieutenant Walter Cox, a doctor who had heard some scuttlebutt that we were investigating the events of December 1966. He is just completing his tour and his DEROS is only a few days away. He explained that, shortly after returning to CONUS, his obligation would be completed and he intended to go into private practice, so he was free to act without fear of retribution. He handed the Flag Lieutenant a sealed manila envelope which he said might be of interest to us. He mentioned that the report inside had been the subject of a massive search by the 'spooks,' but he managed to hide his copy between the pages of an old *Look* magazine. When we opened it we found this." Sergeant Major Sauer removed a single sheet from the envelope, but held it face down on his desk.

"There are seven additional pages, but I must warn you, sir, that the report is highly detailed and immensely disturbing. I'll leave the bulk of the report in the envelope, and you may read it or not as you see fit. I'll also add my notes, and those of MCPON White. But I believe it's the closest we are liable to get to the truth, Captain."

Tom took the report's cover sheet read it silently for several moments, as the others waited respectfully.

OFFICE OF THE CHIEF OF PATHOLOGY
UNITED STATES NAVAL SUPPORT FACILITY
CAMP TIEN SHA
DANANG R.V.N.

15 DEC 1966
Date..........
N--06-1105
Path #..............

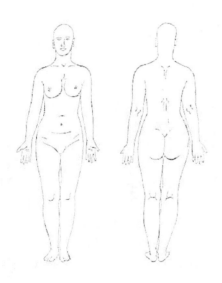

Name: REDACTED **DOB:** REDACTED **S.N:** REDACTED **Gender:** F
Height: 65 Inches **Weight:** 125 Lbs **Race:** Caucasian **Blood Type:** B-
Hair Brown **Eyes:** Green **Identifying Marks:** Tattoos Pig, Left Ankle
approx 2 inches square; Chicken, Right Ankle approx 2 inches square

[ed. note: The complete report may be found in the appendix to this volume.]

"It's her," Tom said sadly. "This is my daughter, Mary Kay Carpentier."

Admiral Tomsen spoke for the others. "How can you be sure, Tom? Granted, all the pieces seem to fit but how can you be certain? All of the critical identification details seem to be redacted."

Tom said nothing, but slowly rolled up his left trouser leg. The faint tattoo of a pig was barely visible. He did the same on the right side, and the clear outline of a chicken could be seen. "I had these done back in, oh, 41 or '42 when I was at Argentia. I'm sure all of you remember the old sailor's superstition that the pig and chicken would keep us from sudden death at sea, don't you?"

All three, including Tincan Tomsen, nodded.

"When Mary Kay was three or four, she used to love riding my leg and playing horsey. She never tired of looking at these tattoos. When she was still at Staten Island, she slipped over to lower Manhattan and had the same tattoos inked on herself. At dinner on the last night before she shipped out, she showed them to me. At first, I was irritated that she'd do such a foolish thing, and I chided her for it. But she simply said, 'I did it for you, Dad. I know that where ever I go, these two guys will look out for me. It will be like you are still watching over me, just like you used to do for Mommy and me when I was little.'

There was nothing left to be said. Admiral Tomsen thanked the two most senior enlisted members of their respective services, and asked them to relay his complements to the Chief of Naval Operations. Tom took the manila envelope and returned the cover sheet to the other pages still inside. Together they left the Marine Barracks, Tincan Tomsen for the brief trip back to the Washington Navy Yard, and Tom to a mournful drive back to Catonsville.

CHAPTER 18
WHAT TO DO WITH A DRUNKEN SAILOR

Friday, August 30, 1968 – Baltimore

Tom drove from Washington in a daze, ignoring the steady rain and bumper-to- bumper traffic common to a Friday afternoon. When he reached Baltimore, he stopped again at the 'Twenty-First Amendment Liquor Store' on U.S. Route 40. The rain continued to fall steadily as he entered and asked the clerk if they sold Scotch by the case.

"Planning a party, hon?" The blowzy blond clerk inquired in a broad South Baltimore accent.

"Not a party exactly. More of a memorial," he replied. Shrugging, the clerk pointed toward a stack of cartons in the rear of the shop. After checking what was available, he selected a case of Johnnie Walker Black Label and carried it to the front.

"Well, the mourners will be happy with your selection," the clerk joked. "If you want cheaper whiskey, we've got Four Roses and Old Crow over there by the beer coolers, and I think there's still some Wild Turkey somewhere back in the storeroom. If you ask me nice, hon, I might go back and fetch you some."

Tom shook his head, but said nothing. Shrugging again, the clerk rang up the sale.

"If you want some company on a rainy afternoon in Bawl'mer, I get off at five. We can make a night of it."

Tom declined, firmly but politely. He returned his car and completed the short drive to his condo. When he entered, he placed the case of liquor on a side table, opened the Venetian blinds to capture whatever light he could, and sat at the kitchen table and opened the manila envelope. He read each page silently, forcing himself to continue. When he finished he placed the papers neatly back into the envelope.

He sat there, his mind in turmoil, until the light began to fade. Learning of his daughter's death while at sea eighteen months before had filled him with crushing sadness; learning now *how* she had died filled him with overwhelming anger and blinding rage. He turned on two small lamps, one in the bedroom and one in the bathroom. He turned off every other light, telephoned the housekeeping service which tended to the condo and discontinued the cleaning service for a week, then disconnected the telephone jack and removed the first bottle of Johnnie Walker from the case. He had no ice cubes, nor tumblers, nor any other kind of barware. All he had, and all he required, was a single common drinking glass.

As a mariner, he had spent as much time ashore in seaman's dives as anyone else. He was no stranger to Scotch whiskey nor its cumulative effects, and estimated that the case should last him a week or more. He drank steadily throughout the evening and into the night. As he did so he began to recall those days long ago, when his little girl used to wait on the pier for her daddy. In his mind's eye, he could see her yet again, first as an infant in her mother's arms, bundled tightly against the biting winds and blowing snow of Newfoundland's south coast. He could see her again as a toddler, her tiny legs struggling to hold her up against the autumn winds, peering up toward the bridge of his destroyer. He saw her still again as a young girl and as a young woman, in New Orleans and St. John's, her eyes dancing with joy at the thought that her dad had, at long last, come home. In those days there were tears of joy, but this night there was no joy. The tears were tears of sadness, tears of loss, tears of rage and anger for what they had done to Mary Kay.

He could hear her voice, too, clearly. The first babble of baby talk: "Daddy boat come home!" and later the excited squeals of "Daddy! Daddy'" when he finally crossed the brow and walked up the pier. He could hear her voice as a schoolgirl chattering on about what had happened that day in school as if, perhaps, after many months as a mate on a freighter, he could somehow keep straight the names of all her little classmates. And when her mother had taken her back to her native island, he remembered her voice, now with a distinct Newfoundland lilt, bragging to her friends that her father was an ocean-going skipper, and not just an ordinary in-shore fisherman. And as the shadows of the day lengthened, he could see her yet again – see her smile, feel her love for animals large or small – and once more know her love for her mother and their love for him.

As the moon became full, and the bottle empty, he rose and navigated himself to his bed. The dim light reflected off the green walls of his bed-room, and the red curtains of the bath. As a mariner, as a ship's captain, it seemed only right that his apartment follow the common maritime rules of the road. As he drifted off into into his whiskey-induced stupor he found himself reciting "Red, Right When Returning From the Sea," over and over again as if somehow the seaman's mantra would bring his only child safely back to him. But he knew – knew with overwhelming, devastating, clarity – that such a thing could never be.

The clock read 3:20 when Tom finally awoke. He had no idea if it was 3:20 AM or 3:20 PM, or even if this were Saturday or some other day in the week, not that it made much difference. He arose and used the bathroom then grabbed a quick shower. Drying off, he slipped into the same rumpled clothes which he had worn previously but had left strewn throughout the bedroom when he finally descended into oblivion.

Opening the bedroom door, he could see light faintly through the Venetian blinds. "That settles that," he thought to himself groggily, "It's 1520 hours, and not 0320. I suppose that's good to know."

He popped two pieces of bread into the toaster and made a pot of coffee. He checked the freezer; there were plenty of TV dinners left. "No need to go out for a while" he thought. "That's good."

He looked at the case of scotch. There was one slot empty, a reminder of the previous night's excesses. "I don't need a clock, I can pretty well tell time by looking at the state of my booze supply," he thought. He removed a second bottle, and poured the first drink of the day.

That day – and the many days which followed – was very much like the first. He drank to forget, but he never forgot to drink. He drank to forget, but the memories refused to be silent. And after a few days the nightmares began. They followed the same pattern always; his daughter was in mortal peril, and he could not save her. Sometimes the dream took place in New Orleans, other times in Newfoundland. Sometimes wild animals pursued her; other times she was walking by a pond or a stream and tumbled in. In all those dreams, he was safe ashore, trying desperately to reach her with a pole or a rope which was always too short. Sometimes he dreamed of fire, other times of flood. In many of the dreams her mother was with them. She berated Tom for his failure to save Mary Kay. "It's your fault, you bastard; you gave me only one child and you couldn't even protect her. You were always too busy to be with your family, Tom. Always off on new adventures, always at sea. I even let you send her to school in the States. Even your vaunted Navy couldn't protect her!"

166

By the time there he was down to the last row of bottles, Tom could tell how long he had slept by the level of pounding in his head. He awoke one morning to search desperately for Excedrin in the medicine cabinet. It took him a few minutes to recognize that this morning's pounding was not just in his head but also on his front door. "Tom, Tom! For God's sake open up! We know you're in there, we can see your car in the parking lot. Tom! Tom Carpentier, open the goddamn door!"

Tom staggered to the door, ragged and disheveled. "Go away! Whoever you are, go away now!"

"Tom, it's me, Becky, Becky Franks. Admiral Tomsen is here with me. Don't make us break down this door! Open the door, Tom, we've been worried sick about you. Admiral Tomsen told me about the meeting at the Marine Barracks."

Tom opened the door.

Admiral Tomsen exclaimed, "Good God, Tom! You look terrible. I was afraid you would do something like this, and when I couldn't reach you by phone I called Becky, wondering if she knew where you might be. She raced down here, and I met her outside. That's where we spotted your car, and to tell you the truth, at first we really feared the worst. But we could hear you moving around and the water running so we knew you must be inside. You gave us a hell of a scare," Tincan Tomsen said.

"What day is it?" Tom asked groggily. "It's Saturday, eight days after I left you at the Marine Barracks. Have you been holed-up here the whole time?"

Tom said nothing. "Well, judging from the state of the apartment and the state that you're in, and by that dwindling case of Johnnie Walker over there on the table, I can see you've at least had a sailor's best friend with

167

you over the past week. But that's not the answer, and you know it's not the answer. Go get cleaned up, and Becky and I will attend to this mess you've been living in."

Tom did as Tincan ordered. Even a retired Vice Admiral still could exercise the voice of command. After a long and very hot shower – longer and hotter by far than he ever could have taken aboard ship – Tom changed into fresh clothes and returned to the living room/kitchen.

Becky greeted her newly resurrected friend. "Admiral Tomsen told me everything, Tom. I cannot even begin to comprehend how you must have felt when you read that report. But getting wasted and going on a week-long bender isn't the way to cope with her death, Tom, and you know that. When I was falling apart after hearing Admiral Topp and hearing everything that Mr. Daley told us, you were there for me. And Admiral Tomsen and I will be here for you."

"Tom, I know you're Roman Catholic. I 'dig with the other foot,' but I know that sometimes it helps Catholics to talk to a priest who understands what you are going through. Becky told me that you ran into the Kerrigan brothers some time ago. I don't support their anti-war rhetoric, but I do give them credit for standing up for what they believe in. If you like, I'll call the one that lives here in Baltimore and you and he can have a chat. I really think that's something you might want to do, shipmate."

Tom nodded, warily. "I may just do that myself, Tincan. There was a priest in Newfoundland, a Father Ed Quinn, who was very consoling when we first got the word. It probably won't hurt."

Tincan looked around the apartment and found the wire for the telephone. When he plugged it back into the answering machine, the recorder began to blink. There were nine calls on the tape. Becky looked at the machine and laughed. "You can ignore at least five of those, Tom. They were from me, and you will be able to tell by my increasing anxiety what this last week was like for me."

"Yeah, and a bunch of them are from me. You really had us worried. But let's get some real chow into you, Tom. Want to head over to Kavanaugh's?"

"Works for me. I'll clear the answering machine when I get back."

After a gargantuan lunch (Tom scoffed down twice as much as he normally would, but then again, it had been a week or more since his last real meal), they returned to his condo. Tom took the remaining four bottles of Johnnie Walker, and gave two to each of his rescuers. "I won't be needing these now. The one thing you learn after spending a lifetime at sea is how to survive a good binge. I'm finished now; you don't need to worry about me."

CHAPTER 19
VENGEANCE IS MINE, SAITH THE LORD

Sunday, September 1, 1968 – Baltimore

After his friends had both departed, Tom checked his messages. As he expected, most of the messages were from Becky or Tincan, and it was clear from the escalating sense of urgency that they both shared a growing concern for his well-being. He erased them all, leaving a single message on the machine. He could tell from the 709 area code that it came from Newfoundland. He just wasn't ready for the conversation which he knew that he must eventually have with his wife.

While he was at the telephone, he dialed 411 and ask the information operator for the telephone number of St. Peter Claver Catholic Church on Fairmount Street in West Baltimore. Retrieving the number, he dialed and ask for Father Phil Kerrigan. When the middle-aged priest came online, Tom introduced himself and explained the purpose of his call. "I'm a merchant mariner, and recently I've been transporting war materials from the U.S. to Vietnam. I know that you and your brother have some very strong views about the Vietnam war, and I'm increasingly concerned about how it is affecting me. Might I stop by and visit with you at your convenience?"

"You may, indeed. It's rather late in the afternoon now, and I have commitments for this evening, and of course for tomorrow morning. Priests never get a Sunday off, especially in small, poor inner-city parishes, after all. But how about tomorrow afternoon, let's say around 2:00 PM? It's easy to find St. Peter's, we're right on Fairmount. Where are you coming from?"

"Well, don't read too much into this, but I'm temporarily staying in Catonsville."

Father Kerrigan chuckled. "Well, it is definitely better for you to visit me than for me to visit you right now! Just come down Frederick Road, and you won't miss us. I'll look for you at two."

Tom retired early, and for the first time since the meeting at the Marine Barracks, slept soundly and without need of 'Dutch Courage.' He arose the next morning and again took a long, hot therapeutic shower, before leaving for the short journey to St. Peter's Church.

He rang the doorbell, and was mildly surprised to be greeted by Father Kerrigan himself. "We're a very poor parish, Tom," the priest explained. "We don't have a housekeeper, and we can't afford a parish secretary. You see, all of our parishioners here are African-American. People may be surprised at the relatively large percentage of black families in Baltimore who are Roman Catholic. It's much higher than in other cities along the East Coast. It may have something to do with Josephite and Glenmary missionaries who came here in the last century, I suppose."

Father Kerrigan showed Tom into a combination office/sitting room. "Would you care for some coffee or tea?"

"No, thank you, Father. I'm afraid that I was deliberately vague about my situation when I talked with you yesterday. While it's true that I am a ship's captain for the Sykes Brother's line, my real reason for coming to see

172

you is this." He handed the tall affable priest the Manila envelope containing the autopsy and investigative reports. Father Kerrigan reviewed them thoughtfully.

After he had completed the last page, Tom said to him, simply, "She was my daughter."

"I'm terribly sorry for your loss, Captain. In times like these, words are completely inadequate, but is there some way that I can help you get through all of this?"

"May I 'open my kimono' with you, Father, as they say in Japan?"

Father Kerrigan laughed softly. "In the seminary, we were taught to call that 'baring my soul', although I must admit that your phrase is much more picturesque. But indeed you may, Captain. Are you a professing Roman Catholic? If so, I can also offer you the opportunity for a spiritual confession, if you think that might be helpful."

"I am, Father, although I don't know that it would be particularly appropriate at the moment. You see, it's not a sin that I *have* committed that concerns me, but one that I think I may commit. Indeed, it's a sin that I very much would like to commit."

"So I take it that you know this man, the so-called *Giant Panda?*"

"No, nor do I know where to find him, but I do know *how* to find him. And some day soon I'll be sailing again to Vietnam, and I don't think that I can resist the urge to find the bastard and do to him what he did to my only child."

"Well Tom," Father Kerrigan replied, "I commiserate with you thoroughly. What you feel now is a white-hot anger, and your anger is really a desire for revenge. When we react to evil we seek vindication, we seek to make the world right again, we seek justice, if you will. Our Lord felt that way when he encountered the money-changers desecrating the Temple. He felt righteous anger, and perhaps understandably so. And the things which offended him were really of little consequence, especially when compared to the unspeakable evil experienced by your daughter."

"I understand what you are trying to say, Father, but ..."

"But what you must consider is this: What you are considering is even a greater sin than what he did to your daughter, because you are premeditating and planning an act of injustice. When you plan to use physical force, even for restoring justice, it may not include injury and death, because life is the Creator's gift to each of us, and no one can morally take away that which is not ours to give."

"You see, Captain, Christian charity requires that we desire what is good, especially the ultimate good which is the salvation for every human being, no matter how despicable or vile the acts of that individual might be."

"She was my only child, Father."

The priest nodded, but then continued.

"Sometimes we forget that any sort of an attempt to redress our injustices by violence just means really that are in denial; denial of God and his nonviolence toward us, denial of the love of our neighbor, denial of the fundamental laws which are essential to our being, Tom," he continued.

"Let me ask you this, Tom. Do you think that something like this could have happened at any other place, at any other time? Today, at this very hour, we are in the process of killing thousands of people – men and

174

women who loved and were loved, the sons and daughters of loving families – and we do it every single day. Josef Stalin has been quoted as saying 'The death of a single person is a tragedy; the death of a million is just a statistic.' And Dorothy Day, of the Catholic Worker's movement once said, 'If I look just at the masses, I will never act'."

Tom nodded, but from politeness only. "Those are two names I never thought I'd hear quoted in the same sentence, Father."

"Beginning in the Middle Ages, Tom, the Church attempted to develop a systematic approach to help determine when war is justified." The priest handed Tom a worn piece of paper:

$$* \quad * \quad *$$

Jus ad Bellum- The Just War:

Just Cause: War is permissible only to confront "a real and certain danger," i.e. to protect innocent life, to preserve conditions necessary for decent human life existence, and to protect basic human rights.

Competent Authority: The right to use force must be joined with the common good; war must be declared by those with responsibility for public order, not by private groups or individuals.

Comparative Justice: No state should act on the basis that it has "absolute justice" on its side. Every party to a conflict must acknowledge the limits of its "just cause" and the consequent requirement to use only limited means in pursuit of its objectives.

Right Intention: War can be legitimately intended for only the reasons set forth as a just cause.

Last Resort: *For war to be justified, all peaceful alternatives must have been exhausted.*

Probability of Success: *This is a difficult criterion to apply, but its purpose is to prevent irrational resort to force or hopeless resistance when the outcome of either will clearly be disproportionate or futile.*

Proportionality: *The destruction to be inflicted and the costs incurred by war must be proportionate to the good expected by taking up arms. Destruction applies in both the temporal and spiritual sense.*

Discrimination: *This criterion requires that actions within a war must never be "total war", and must never target civilian populations or non-military targets.*

✻　✻　✻

"When this war in Vietnam began under President Kennedy, I used to ask my students which of these points might justify sending our troops into this conflict. Now, I defy anyone to identify even one of these points we *haven't* violated, over and over in Southeast Asia. Not even one, Tom."

"And I'm sure you've read in the newspapers of the young American Lieutenant at My Lai who lost control of his platoon, a few months ago, and killed nearly 300 innocent civilians. You yourself told me that you sail to Vietnam with cargoes of bullets and shells and the mechanisms to fire them. Where do you think they go, Tom? We Catholics hide behind what we consider this 'doctrine of the just war.' That's nothing but Jesuitical word-smithing, a simple checklist, if you will, that helps us in taking innocent lives in the name of our government. It assuages our consciences, and helps sleep better at night, I suppose."

"Yet at the same time we pray '*From the famine, pestilence, and war: Oh Lord, do thou deliver us.*' Don't you think that the Catholics among the Vietnamese pray the same prayer? Does it really matter if the bombs you so carefully bring across 12,000 miles of ocean fall on Catholics, or Buddhists or non-believers? They're all gooks, or slope-heads or dinks, aren't they? First we rob them of their human dignity through our words; then we rob them of life itself through our actions."

"Tell me, Tom, do you really believe that what you are considering will end well? I am terribly sorry for your loss, and the horrific fate which befell your daughter. I will pray for you and your family. But I think you know the answer to your quandary, Tom. No action that you could ever take will restore your daughter to you. But it's how you act now that will restore some small sense of decency to the world in which we live. I pray that you make the right choice, my friend."

Tom thanked him for his insight and drove back to Catonsville. For a moment he thought about detouring to the liquor store on Route 40 but resisted the temptation. When he returned home the red light on the answering machine was blinking urgently.

CHAPTER 20
A DOOR OPENS

Tuesday, September 10, 1968 – Danang RVN

Tom was surprised to hear the voice of Commodore Roy Fontenot on his answering machine. Sykes Brothers prided itself on not interfering with the limited amount of time its mariners were able to spend ashore.

"Tom, I need to talk to you. I tried calling your father-in-law in Newfoundland, but he said that you had returned stateside a few weeks ago. Please, regardless of when you get this, give me a call either at home or at the office. I really need to talk to you."

Tom looked at his watch. It was nearly 5 PM. He opened his wallet and retrieved the Commodore's home telephone number. Roy Fontenot was the most senior captain currently active with Sykes Brothers; the title of Commodore was an honorific traditionally bestowed on the most experienced ship's captain of any fleet. Tom dialed the Commodore's number. "Hello sir, I understand you're trying to reach me. Is everything okay?"

"Thanks for getting back to me Tom. We're in the midst of a minor crisis here, and I think you can help us out."

"What's up, Commodore?"

"Well, your relief on the *Rita E*, Jacques La Ochdha, suffered a moderate-to-severe stroke last Thursday evening. He'd been having a difficult voyage; he had to run well to the north after leaving Pearl Harbor to avoid Typhoon Helene, so he lost about 72 hours waiting until he could skirt around and get behind the storm. But he encountered some heavy weather on the fringes, and the boatswain, Jesse Orwin, slipped and broke a leg. Not only that but the donkeyman got whacked badly by a timber beam that had gone adrift. He suffered a concussion, but we think he'll be okay. All this happened because whoever supervised the stowage of cargo at Honolulu left the ship terribly out of balance. Several of the temporary bulkheads in holds three and four cracked, and they've got cargo sliding everywhere. With the boatswain out of commission, and the donkeyman somewhat the worse for wear, I could see why La Ochdha was feeling stressed. They found him in his cabin, unable to speak or move and called for an evacuation helicopter. But the combination of their position and the crappy weather made the Coast Guard duty officer feel that the better option would be to offload him at the next port, which is Subic Bay."

"I think I can see where this is going, sir."

"Yeah. Joe Roy, your first mate is doing a bang up job keeping things under control. I don't believe the *Rita E* is in any serious difficulty, but I will feel a lot better with a master mariner on the deck. That's where you come in. Given the current conditions, the *Rita E* ought to make Subic Bay in about 96 hours. Subic Bay is jammed up; the last I heard they had about 50 ships lying at anchor out in the roadstead. We're talking to the Coast Guard now to see if they could declare an emergency for us, which would get us to the top of the queue, and get us alongside some time Friday afternoon, Philippine time. I hate to ask you this, but I really need you to get over there as quickly as you can. The deal I have for you is that we'll take your remaining shore leave time and double it. We'll also pay you danger money from the time you leave Subic until the time you clear Vietnam on the way back, rather than just when you're inside the 12 mile limit off RVN. It appears that

180

you will be headed back stateside pretty much in ballast, unless we pick up a load at Danang, which is highly unlikely. Can you help me out, Tom?"

"I'll be happy to, Commodore. With the exception of a second dental appointment, which I can easily postpone, I don't have anything on the calendar for the next few weeks."

"Your a good shipmate, Tom. I kept telling Jacques that if he didn't take better care of his health, one of these days he was going to drop dead. He smokes about a box of Phillies Blunts every week, and he has the cook make him a dozen donuts by 0600 every morning when he comes on watch. The only exercise he gets is jumping to conclusions, which he may have done when he signed off on the third mate's weight and balance calculations before they headed out of Pearl. Joe Roy told me on the radiophone that Jacques's whole right side is paralyzed. Our in-house doctor here also spoke to Joe several times; things appear to be stable right now, but Doc says you never know which way these kinds of things are going to go. Both he and I will feel a lot better if we can get him into the Public Health Service hospital back in Honolulu. I'm going to set up a Medevac flight to get him back to Hawaii as quickly as possible once they arrive at Subic Bay."

"Can you give me a little help with the logistics?"

"I'm one step ahead of you on that Tom. We contacted our agent there in Baltimore this morning. As soon as you get off of this call, call him. He'll arrange airline tickets and a cash advance, and make sure your documents are all in order. I'll tell you what: Let him know that you and I spoke, and that I authorize a first-class ticket from Baltimore to the Philippines. It's the least we can do."

"Thank you, sir, that's most decent of you. Incidentally, did I hear you say Danang a minute or so ago?"

"Yeah, the Military Sea Transportation Service changed the orders about two weeks ago. The *Rita E* was originally scheduled for Cam Ranh Bay, but they shifted us north to get material to the Marines more quickly. Ever since the Tet Offensive back in February, things are hopping in the north, and this saves several days when they won't need multiple convoys heading up through Indian country. You'll go right up the Han River and dock at an old French Wharf in the heart of the old city. I was in there myself on the *Mimi M* a couple years ago. It's a good safe anchorage, and they usually turn the ship before you tie up. That will give you about a 16 km run until you make open water when you depart. I'll have to check; I'm not sure if we will bring you in to Tacoma or some other port on the West Coast. Tacoma gives you the best and shortest great-circle run stateside; it saves about a day over San Pedro, and saves us a lot of fuel besides."

"Okay, Commodore. Let me get started on things and your agent will be able to let you know my travel schedule. And give my regards to old Jacques La Ochdha. There is nothing like lying on your back partially paralyzed to sound a wake-up call about watching your weight."

Tom hung up from his call with Commodore Fontenot, and immediately contacted the ship's agent in Baltimore. True to his word, Commodore Fontenot had made the necessary arrangements, and by the middle of the next afternoon, Tom was on a United flight from Baltimore to Seattle, with a connecting flight on Northwest Orient to Manila. The first-class accommodations were excellent, and Tom slept most of the way on each leg of the flight. Less than 36 hours after departure, he arrived in the Philippines, and the local agent transported him to the Naval base at Subic Bay.

Tom was on the dock when the *Rita E.* arrived on Friday morning, as were two ambulances, representatives of the Military Sea Transportation Service and the Sykes Brothers Shipping Line, and a crew of local dock workers. As the brow came across, paramedics were the first to board and soon had Jacques bundled into an ambulance. A few minutes later, Jesse

Orwin, his leg bound tightly into a splint, was assisted off the ship by another crew of medics. Finally the donkeyman, (whose given name was Sokratis Liberopoulos, and who definitely preferred his job title to his nickname 'Liverwurst') walked down the gangway under his own power. Tom took advantage of the short break in the action to haul his sea bag and suitcases aboard before the dock workers clambered up the gangway.

He was met by Joe Roy as he crossed the deck. Joe appeared exhausted.

"Had a lovely trip, I take it?" Tom asked sardonically.

"One more week like this, skipper, and I'm headed back to Thibodaux. A nice quiet shrimper in a Gulf hurricane would be a major improvement over the trip here from Pearl Harbor. As my old grandpappy used to say 'if it ain't one thing, it's two things.' Actually, it was about two dozen things."

"Well, since you just cleared the binnacle list, I guess the next thing on the agenda will be to attend to this issue of cargo stowage. I watched you as you came alongside the pier but I couldn't detect any list. Did you guys manage to get it under control?"

"No, we still have a lot of material that has come unstowed, particularly in the second and third holds. I'm about to murder Frannie Browne, the third mate. He gave Jacques a totally bogus weight and balance calculation. He used one of those new-fangled electronic calculators that everybody's talking about. Personally, I like to figure things manually, the same way we've always done from the time of the Phoenicians. But these kids figure their 'goes-inta' is better and faster than the way we old-timers do it, and I suppose he may be right, if you load the correct numbers in there in the first place. But 'garbage in-garbage out' seems to apply in this case. I did confiscate his calculator however, and if I don't toss it over the side, I'll give it back to him when we reach stateside."

Tom laughed. "You might want to take away his sextant, and let him use a lodestone for a while. That ought to teach him."

They retired to the bridge, and Tom reviewed the logs, from the time he left the ship in early July, until the time it berthed that morning. Aside from the shifting cargo, which the dock workers were preparing to correct at the moment, the voyage was essentially unremarkable. "When are we due out of here, Joe?" Tom asked.

"The typhoon slowed us down considerably, skipper. We're about 72 hours behind schedule, so if you can get us out of here by tomorrow morning, and the load is stable, we should make up some time en route to Vietnam. We've been diverted from Cam Ranh up to Danang, so we should save some time there. It's about 1300 km between here and Danang; at 15 knots average it ought to take us about 45 hours. If we bail out of here tomorrow morning before 1000 hrs. we ought to be in Danang by 0700 Monday morning. Depending on congestion at the wharves, we ought to begin unloading some time late Monday, or more likely on Tuesday. Given all the cargo we've picked up on the way over, we should be totally unloaded and ready to get out of there not much later than Thursday."

Tom glanced down to the weather deck. "I see the MSTS representative talking to our agent. I'm going to wander down there and see what they have to say."

Tom learned that they would receive priority both at Subic Bay and at Danang due to the critical need for the materials they had on board. He returned to the bridge and told Joe that it looked like this would be a 'Red Ball express'. Joe, a veteran of Patton's Third Army. winced. "That's all I need," he said, laughing.

The expedited repairs and re-stowing of material went as planned and they were able to get off the dock at Subic on schedule. For once, the forecast for the South China Sea was favorable, light winds and Sea State 2 or below for the entire two-day trip across to Danang. Tom used the time to stow his gear and to generally re-acquaint himself with the *Rita E*. To be honest, he felt better now that he was back at sea than he had ashore. This had not been the most restful shore leave that he'd ever experienced.

They reached Danang on schedule, and proceeded up the Han River to the turning pool. The Vietnamese pilot was obviously competent, having handled a vast number of ships since the war began in 1964. By noon on Sunday, they were tied 'port-side to' at wharf number three, about halfway between the mouth of the river and the bridge linking Danang City with Camp Tien Sha below Monkey Mountain. Their unloading was delayed, however, by a shortage of mobile cranes and did not begin until early Thursday morning. Once unloading began, though, it went quickly. By 0900 the following morning, they were ready to leave and the port controller scheduled their departure for high tide shortly after 1300 hrs.

When Tom received word of their scheduled departure, he returned to his cabin and locked the door. Inside the cabin, as in every skipper's cabin of the Sykes Brothers line, stood a small safe containing, among other things, a supply of cash, critical ship's documents, and a .45 caliber pistol and three clips of ammunition. Tom opened the safe, removed the cash and the weapon as well as the spare clips and re-locked it. He inserted a clip in the weapon, pulled back the slide to chamber a round, and clicked the safety to the 'off' position. He then changed into his formal uniform, complete with raincoat as protection against the steady drizzle. He walked out to the main weather deck, where Joe Roy was supervising the last of the unloading.

"I'm going over to the MSTS office to attend to some last-minute paper-work," he said to Joe, showing him the manila envelope he had carried all the way from Baltimore. "I believe it's over at the Naval Support Activity office in that large white building about a quarter of a mile up the road. Take care of things for me, will you, Joe? It may be some time until I return."

Entrance to the White Elephant Facility in Danang, RVN in 1968

CHAPTER 21
FINAL DEPARTURES

Saturday, September 14, 1968 – Pacific Ocean

Joe Roy stood on the port-side wing of the *Rita E*. The Vietnamese pilot was already aboard; all hatch covers had been dogged down tightly, and the lines holding the ship to the wharf had been singled up. *The Rita E*, in all aspects save one, was ready for sea.

The ship's radioman, Dom Rossi, came out on the bridge wing. "We just had a radio call from the port controller across the river at Camp Tien Sha. He has a Harrison Line freighter coming up river now and heading for the turning basin. As soon as he passes us, we can shove off, but the port controller warned us that the Harrison boat will be coming in behind us to tie up at this wharf within the next 30 minutes. Time to head back to the barn, Mate."

"We'll get underway as soon as the skipper gets back on board," Joe related. "He's over at the Naval Support Activity headquarters building, the one they call the White Elephant, and should be back here momentarily. I have a dock crew ready to pull back the brow and toss off the lines and then we are out of here."

Joe Roy continued to look at his watch every few minutes. "Where the hell is the skipper? He knew we were going to be out of here at 1300 hours; I wonder what's keeping him?

Finally, a few minutes after 1300, Joe spotted the captain walking slowly toward the ship. Irritated by the delay, and with the Harrison boat now turned and heading back down river, Joe thought to himself, "Ah, for God's sake, Tom, speed it up, would you? The last captain was slow, but he weighed 250 pounds. Come on – you're not still on shore leave, skipper!"

Tom finally reached the gangway and came aboard. Joe went to the main deck to welcome him and brief him on their current status. Before he could speak, the skipper shook his head. He was dripping wet and deathly pale.

"We're ready to..." Joe started.

"I'm going to my cabin. You have the conn, Joe. Get us the hell out of here and let me know when we are in international waters."

"Are you sure, Tom?"

"Joe, just do it."

Tom proceeded to his cabin, removed his dripping raincoat, and sat at his desk. In a trance-like state, he removed the .45 caliber pistol from his pocket and placed it on the desk in front of himself. He could feel the throbbing of the engines as they maneuvered away from the wharf.

After several hours, Joe Roy knocked firmly on the cabin door. "Are you okay, skipper? Anything going on?"

Hearing no reply, he opened the door. Tom was still sitting silently at his desk.

"Skipper, are you okay? You look terrible. You're deathly pale, and your hands are trembling. Did something happen over at the White Elephant?"

Tom handed Joe Roy the envelope which he had carried since he left Baltimore. Joe sat across from Tom, opened it and read the contents.

"My God, skipper, we didn't know. This is about your daughter, isn't it?" He moved forward in his chair and subtly moved the .45 caliber pistol to his side of the desk.

"I saw her Joe. I saw her as clearly as I see you now. She was closer to me than I am to you. I saw her, Joe."

"You had a vision, Tom?" Joe asked.

"No, Joe you don't understand. *I-saw-her.*"

"And where did you see her, Tom?"

Tom sighed. "I had gone across to the White Elephant intending to kill the bastards who raped and murdered my daughter. I told the gate guard I was going to the MSTS office, but when I got in the building I turned down the corridor leading to the Air America wing. I knew I wouldn't get out of the building alive, but I just didn't care any more. I just wanted this pain to stop, Joe. But as I reached the end of the corridor, she was standing there. Mary Kay was standing there, Joe, in her dress blue Navy uniform. I had the gun in the pocket of my raincoat, loaded and with the safety off. I was going to kill those sons of bitches. I could have reached out and touched her, Joe. She was that close. And Mary Kay spoke to me. 'No,

Daddy, don't. It's okay, I'm in a better place. Please, Daddy, go home to Mommy. She needs you. We will be together again before long, I promise.' And then she turned the corner and walked away."

Tom Carpentier and Joe Roy sat together quietly as at dusk overtook the *Rita E.* For a long period – perhaps a few minutes, perhaps hours, who knows? – they said nothing; there was nothing to say. Finally Joe asked, "Would you like something to drink Tom? I know where the deck gang hide their duty-free stash. They won't miss a bottle or two."

"No, I had enough of that before I left Baltimore. I know you think I'm delusional, Joe, and that I had an hallucination or some sort of a vision, but no, she was *there* Joe. And after she turned and left I took out the .45 and held it in my hand. I know what a .45 can do at close range, and to be honest, Joe, I was about to turn it on myself. But then I thought about what she said. *'Please, Daddy, go home to Mommy. She needs you.'*"

Joe Roy calmly took the pistol, removed the clip, cleared the chamber, and placed it in his own pocket.

"You don't have to worry about that, Joe. I'm okay now."

"We've just past the outer marker for the Han River channel, skipper. We're in open waters and we're headed home. Get some sleep, Tom. I can handle things until you feel more up to it."

"Thanks, Joe, you're a real shipmate. I'll be okay in a little while. I have some thinking to do and some decisions to make."

Later that evening, Tom went to the bridge and surveyed the ship's situation. Aside from some minor vibration, everything seemed to be under control. He signaled Joe to come out on the starboard wing of the bridge, out of earshot of the wheelman and other unlicensed crewmen on the bridge.

He handed the first mate a sealed envelope, bearing the crest of the Sykes Brothers Shipping line. "Do me a favor, Joe. When we get stateside, would you deliver this to Captain Fontenot for me? I'm swallowing the anchor, my friend, and in this letter I recommend that you take command of the *Rita E.* It's time for me to move on, Joe."

The voyage across the Pacific was uneventful, save for a recurring squeal which the engineer diagnosed as a failing bearing deep in the shaft-alley, and which was no doubt responsible for the ship's vibrations. After a flurry of messages, the home office in New Orleans diverted them from Tacoma to the Fairhaven repair facility in Bellingham, some 120 miles north. Shortly after they arrived, Tom, his bags already packed, shook hands with Joe Roy. "Smooth sailing, Mate. I'll see you again somewhere," he said, as he slowly crossed gangway for the last time.

He hailed a taxi for the short ride up the Pacific Coast Highway to the border control point at Blaine and, after passing through the American side, entered Canada at Surrey, British Columbia. "Have you anything to declare?" asked the representative of the Canadian government.

"Yes, I'm an American citizen," Tom replied, presenting his documents, including his Master Mariner's License. "I oppose the war in Vietnam, and I would like to apply for status as a landed immigrant in Canada. I intend to apply for Canadian citizenship at the earliest opportunity." After some perfunctory questions, which Tom answered honestly and fully, and after recording the many temporary entrance stamps for trips to and from Newfoundland, the immigration official reached into his desk and withdrew an old-fashioned hand-stamp, which he applied to the last full page of Tom's passport:

Immigrant Reçu
Application for Permanent Status Pending

"Welcome to Canada, Skipper. We're happy to have you," the official declared, and reached out to shake his hand.

CHAPTER 22
HOME IS THE SAILOR

His newly approved residency documents in hand, Tom summoned a taxi to continue his short trip to Vancouver. He asked to be deposited at Waterfront Station on West Cordova Street, the downtown terminus of the Canadian Pacific Railway. While most passengers might perceive a sea voyage to be relaxing, it is never really possible for a ship's captain to feel fully at ease while his ship as at sea. Things can turn from humdrum to horrific in a single moment, as seafarers from Odysseus to Captain Cook have learned to their dismay. Tom looked forward to several days of relaxation and the opportunity to see much more of his newly adopted country than he had seen to date. He purchased first-class tickets from Vancouver to Toronto, a journey which would take him through some of the most scenic, and also some of the most barren, areas of Canada.

The trip across Canada was indeed as relaxing and restorative as Tom had hoped. The dining car food and the service provided by the cheerful train attendants aboard Canadian Pacific's crack flagship train *The Canadian* were excellent, and his small roomette was warm and comfortable. He left the train for about an hour at each stop in Calgary, Regina, Winnipeg and Sudbury (where it was snowing heavily). He enjoyed the quick views of four very different cities and was in excellent spirits when he arrived in Toronto three days later, where he purchased a one-way ticket to St. John's on Eastern Provincial Airways. He had not spoken to his wife nor her father since leaving Baltimore, preferring to first consult Loretta before announcing his life-changing decision to her entire family.

After extensive deliberation, on his last night aboard the *Rita E,* he had burned every document provided to him by Admiral Moore's staff. He did not intend to share any of the disturbing details with anyone, not even with Mary Kay's mother. "It's a secret best taken to my grave," he thought to himself. He arrived in Saint John's later that afternoon, and Loretta was delighted with his unexpected visit. She was even more pleased when he showed her the final page in his American passport.

"I am Canadian now," he announced to her family at dinner, "or at least I will be in three years when I can finally apply for full citizenship and declare my allegiance to Queen and Country. This was not a snap decision, there are many reasons why I took this step, but let's not go into those now. I have resigned my position with Sykes Brothers Line and I suppose that now I'll be what *"we"* Newfoundlanders call an 'angashore' [hang-a-shore], sitting around on my duff all day. I have a substantial severance check as well as a decent pension that will be coming to me in the future. I propose to remain here in Newfoundland for the rest of my life, and I can't think of a single place where I'd rather be."

"Aye, Tom." Loretta's father laughed, "you may just be the first person I've ever met to make that decision individually. All of us in Newfoundland became Canadian at the same time, on July 1, 1949, when Joey Smallwood, 'the only living Father of Confederation' dragged the island into union with the folks up-a-long, although many of us felt at that time that it was *Canada* that was finally wising up and joining up with Newfoundland. But there is no doubt that conditions have certainly improved substantially on the island over the past twenty years or so."

Tom and Loretta spent several weeks relaxing and becoming re-accustomed to married life. They bought matching snowmobiles and traveled throughout the Avalon Peninsula. In the spring they found a small house well within their budget, centrally located on Bonaventure Avenue near Holy Heart of Mary High School, where Loretta had taught for many years. It soon became a magnet for gaggles of nieces and nephews of Tom and Loretta's extended family, attracted by Auntie Loretta's baking and Skipper Tom's exciting tales of battling pirates, monsters and an ever-changing cast of sea-serpents in hurricanes, typhoons, and cyclones as he sailed the seven seas for treasure (or at least a positive balance sheet!) for the dauntless Brothers Sykes. Others came to visit too. One summer day in 1971, Becky Franks-Vlanderen and her husband Hans appeared in a Winnebago the size of the old Rita E, with their eleven-month-old son Tommy in tow. Later that summer, Tom and Loretta drove out to Argentia to meet the Tomsens, who had come up on the CN ferry Ambrose Shea for the thirtieth anniversary of the signing of the Atlantic Charter. Tom had invited Tincan to visit, but had asked him to say nothing about their discoveries three years before. And through the influence of his father-in-law, who was well regarded in political circles throughout the province, Tom obtained a position as Professor of Navigation Sciences at the new Fisheries College, part of the Memorial University of Newfoundland. The main campus of Fisheries College was located on Parade Road, and Tom traded his life as skipper of a sea-going freighter for a marginally less harrowing command of a battered second-hand Schwinn three-speed bike, dodging traffic on busy Merrymeeting Road twice daily.

One evening, after many years had passed, Tom and Loretta lingered over their supper, reflecting on the ways that their lives had grown and reconnected. "I don't think I've ever mentioned this to you, Tom, but I knew for certain that you would come back to Newfoundland to stay. One night – I believe it was in September of 1968, I had the most vivid dream imaginable. It was so clear that when I awoke I could not tell if it had been real or just a dream. It was Mary Kay, Tom. I saw her standing at the foot of my bed in her Navy uniform, and she said, 'It's okay Mommy, I spoke to Daddy and he's coming home to you and soon we can all be together forever.' When I awoke I was at first terrified, and then confused, but when I became fully awake, well, I think that that was the first time since we learned of her death that I ever felt truly at peace. I know you think I'm silly, Tom, but that really happened. And wherever our daughter is now, and regardless of what may have happened to her, I'm sure that she's looking over us today. I've kept all these things in my heart, Tom, from that day to this."

Tom said nothing. Once again, there was nothing more to say. But in Newfoundland it is often said: "When love is true, heaven is near." And perhaps it has ever been so.

APPENDICES

APX-001 OFFICERS AND MEN OF USS REUBEN JAMES (DD-245)

This is a true and complete crew-list, extracted from the files of the Bureau of Personnel of the United States Navy. As a result, and to avoid any disrespect to these brave sailors, the name of our fictional character George T. Franks, MM2c is not included

OFFICERS

Lieutenant Commander	Edwards, Heywood Lane, USN
Lieutenant	Ghetzler, Benjamin, USN
Lieutenant	Johnston, Dewey George, USN
Lieutenant (junior grade)	Belden, James Mead, USN
Lieutenant (junior grade)	Daub, John Justus, USN
Ensign	Spowers, Craig, USN
Ensign	Wade, Howard Voyer, USN

CHIEF PETTY OFFICERS

Chief Boarswain's Mate	Devereau, Lawrence Delaney, USN
Chief Carpenter's Mate	Cousins, Alton Adelbert, USN
Chief Carpenter's Mate	Keever, Leonard A., USN
Chief Commissary Steward	French, Ralph George, USN

Chief Electrician's Mate	Greer, John Calvin, USN
Chief Gunner's Mate	Towers, George F., USN
Chief Machinist's Mate	Bergstresser, William Henry, USN
Chief Quartermaster	Jones, Glen W., USN
Chief Radioman	Bauer, John Francis, USN
Chief Torpedoman's Mate	Cox, Charles Beacon, USN
Chief Water Tender	Mondouk, Albert J., USN
Chief Water Tender	Parkin, Joseph J., USN
Chief Water Tender	Schlotthauer, Eugene, USN

PETTY OFFICERS

Water Tender First Class	Long, Gordon H., USN
Boatswain's Mate First Class	Post, Frederick R., USN
Boilerman First Class	Saltis, Edward Peter, USN
Cook First Class	Ortizuela, Pedro, USN
Fire Controlman First Class	Wharton, Kenneth R., USN
Gunner's Mate First Class	Henniger, William Henry, USN
Gunner's Mate First Class	Kapecz, Rudolph T., USN
Machinist's Mate First Class	Boyd, Solon Gescovy, USN
Machinist's Mate First Class	Gaskins, Lester Carson, USN
Machinist's Mate First Class	Gorziza, Arthur Emil, USN
Machinist's Mate First Class	Musslewhite, Edgar W., USN
Machinist's Mate First Class	Westbury, William C., USN
Mess Attendant First Class	Johnson, Joseph, USN
Pharmacist's Mate First Class	Powell, Lee P., USN
Radioman First Class	Magaris, Paul L., USN
Shipfitter First Class	Zapasnik, Fred F., USN
Steward's Mate First Class	Cook, Raymond, USN
Torpedoman's Mate First Class	Reid, Lee Louis N., USN
Water Tender First Class	Doiron, Gilbert Joseph, USN
Water Tender First Class	Sims, Lloyd E., USN
Yeoman First Class	Boynton, Paul Rogers, USN

Boatswain's Mate Second Class	Kalanta, Anthony J., USN
Boilerman Second Class	Evans, Gene Guy, USN
Electrician's Mate Second Class	Turnbull, Thomas P., USN
Fire Controlman Second Class	Clark, James Brantley, USN
Gunner's Mate Second Class	Cosgrove, Lawrence R. USN
Machinist's Mate Second Class	Beasley, George N, USN
Machinist's Mate Second Class	Begley, Claborn, USN
Machinist's Mate Second Class	Benson, James Franklin, USN
Machinist's Mate Second Class	Graham, Guy Shipp, USN
Machinist's Mate Second Class	Hajowy, Joseph, USN
Machinist's Mate Second Class	Stencel, Julius, USNR
Metalsmith First Class	James, Vance Turner, USN
Quartermaster Second Class	Pennington, Burl G., USN
Radioman Second Class	Caruso, Joseph James, USN
Ship's Cook Second Class	Franks, Hartley Hardy, USN
Shipfitter Second Class	Jaeggi, Earl William, USN
Signalman Second Class	Griffin, Arthur Raymond, USN
Torpedoman's Mate Second Class	Flynn, William Aloysius, USN
Electrician's Mate Third Class	Tate, Cleophas, USN
Gunner's Mate Third Class	Cooperider, Carl Eugene, USN
Gunner's Mate Third Class	Hogan, Francis Robert, USN
Gunner's Mate Third Class	House, Hugh, USN
Gunner's Mate Third Class	Sorensen, Walter, USN
Gunner's Mate Third Class	Stewart, Aaron H., USN
Mess Attendant Third Class	Dunston, Nebraska, USN
Quartermaster Third Class	Fitzgerald, John Joseph, USN
Radioman Third Class	Bridges, Brent Neil, USN
Radioman Third Class	Dyson, Corbon, USN
Radioman Third Class	Oaks, Kenneth Courtland, USN
Signalman Third Class	Kloepper, Ralph W.H., USN
Signalman Third Class	Turner, Lewis Aubrey, USN

Storekeeper Third Class	Dickerson, Leonidas USN
Torpedoman's Mate Third Class	Howard, Robert Joseph, USN
Torpedoman's Mate Third Class	Neptune, Aldon W., USN
Yeoman Third Class	Newton, William Harding, USN
Yeoman Third Class	Daniel, Dennis Howard, USN

STRIKERS

Coxswain	Britt, Harold Lelie, USN
Coxswain	Delisle, Gerald Joseph, USN
Coxswain	Paterson, William N., USN
Coxswain	Ryan, John J., USN
Fireman First Class	Carbaugh, Leftwich E, USN
Fireman First Class	Coyle, Floyd Bob, USN
Fireman First Class	Elnitsky, Joseph Fedenich, USN
Fireman First Class	Hingula, Norman Francis, USN
Fireman First Class	Hudlin, Maurice W. USN
Fireman First Class	Jacquette, Charles USN
Fireman First Class	Molnar, Joseph, USN
Fireman First Class	Richardson, Lester E., USN
Fireman First Class	Taylor, Wilton L., USN
Fireman First Class	Vore, Harold M., USN
Fireman Third Class	Evans, Linn Stewart, USN
Seaman First Class	Beasley, Harold Hamner, USN
Seaman First Class	Biehl, Joseph Peter, USN
Seaman First Class	Byrd, Hartwell Lee, USN
Seaman First Class	Del Grosso, Daniel J USN
Seaman First Class	Drinkwalter, Karl Lee, USN
Seaman First Class	Farley, Edwin Louis, USN
Seaman First Class	Gunn, Donald Knapp, USN
Seaman First Class	Little, Joseph Gustave, USN
Seaman First Class	Owen, Benjamin T., USN
Seaman First Class	Painter, William H., USN
Seaman First Class	Polizzi, Joseph C., USN

Seaman First Class	Porter, Corwin D., USN
Seaman First Class	Rayhill, Elmer R., USN
Seaman First Class	Ress, John R., USN
Seaman First Class	Robinson, Clarence F., USN
Seaman First Class	Rogers, James W., USN
Seaman First Class	Rose, Charles Ray, USN
Seaman First Class	Rygwelski, Clarence, USN
Seaman First Class	Settle, Sunny J., USN
Seaman First Class	Sills, Lawrence, USN
Seaman First Class	Stelmach, Jerome, USN
Seaman First Class	Voiles, Loyd Z., USN
Seaman First Class	Weaver, Jesse, USN
Seaman First Class	Woody, George, USN
Seaman First Class	Wray, Edwin E., USN
Fireman Second Class	Appleton, Charlie, USN
Fireman Second Class	Appleton, Parmie, USN
Fireman Second Class	Bush, Roy Virgil, USN
Fireman Second Class	Carr, Robert James, USN
Fireman Second Class	Everett, Carlyle Chester, USN
Fireman Second Class	Giehr, George Frederick, USN
Fireman Second Class	Merrell, Windell Harmon, USN
Fireman Second Class	Olmstead, Donald Everett, USN
Fireman Second Class	Phalen, Charles W., USN
Fireman Second Class	Welch, Chester L., USN
Seaman Second Class	Burrell, Herbert Ralph, USN
Seaman Second Class	Grey, Ernest Dwane, USN
Seaman Second Class	Harris, Charles Waldon, USN
Seaman Second Class	Hayes, Charles Chester, USN
Seaman Second Class	McKeever, William J USN
Seaman Second Class	Merritt, Auburn F., USN
Seaman Second Class	Mills, Gerald Edward, USN
Seaman Second Class	Nagle, Earl G., USN

Seaman Second Class	Neely, Kenneth Cecil, USN
Seaman Second Class	Niece, Delos, USN
Seaman Second Class	Olexa, Steve, USN
Seaman Second Class	Orange, Harold J., USN
Seaman Second Class	Stankus, Anthony G. USN
Seaman Second Class	Stewart, Robert S., USN
Seaman Second Class	Thompson, James C., USN
Seaman Second Class	Sowers, Wallace L., USN
Fireman Third Class	Rodgers, Talmage Roscoe, USN
Fireman Third Class	Tyger, Leland E., USN

APX-002 List Of Clemson-Class Destroyers Transferred to the United Kingdom And to Canada As Part Of The Destroyers-For Bases Agreement Of 1940

TRANSFERRED	RENAMED
USSSatterlee (DD-190)	HMS Belmont
USS Mason (DD-191)	HMS Broadwater
USS Hunt (DD-194)	HMS Broadway
USS Welborn C. Wood	HMS Chesterfield
USS Branch (DD-197)	HMS Beverley
USS Herndon (DD-198)	HMS Churchill
USS McCook (DD-252)	HMCS St Croix
USS McCalla (DD-253)	HMS Stanley
USS Rodgers (DD-254)	HMS Sherwood
USS Bancroft (DD-256)	HMCS St Francis
USS Welles (DD-257)	HMS Cameron
USS Aulick (DD-258)	HMS Burnham
USS Laub (DD-263)	HMS Burwell
USSMcLanahan (DD-264)	HMS Bradford
USS Edwards (DD-265)	HMS Buxton
USS Shubrick (DD-268)	HMS Ripley
USS Bailey (DD-269)	HMS Reading
USS Swasey (DD-273	HMS Rockingham
USS Meade (DD-274)	HMS Ramsey
USS Upshur (DD-193)	HMS Claire

APX-003 ALMANIC DATA REGARDING THE SINKING OF USS REUBEN JAMES DD-245

U.S. Naval Observatory

Date	31.10.41		Lat.	N52.3
U. Time + 2h			Long.	W27.2

SUN

Begin civil twilight	10:06
Sunrise	10:42
Sun transit	15:33
Sunset	20:22
End civil twilight	20:58

MOON

Moonrise	18:54 prev. day
Moon transit	00:42
Moonset	06:39
Moonrise	19:17
Moonset	07:44 next day

Phase of the Moon on 31 October: waxing gibbous with 88% of the Moon's visible disk illuminated.

Full Moon 4 November 1941 at 04:00 (Universal Time + 2h).

[ed note. Discrepancies between reported times between German and Allied reported times due to German usage of Middle European Time (GMT+2) and Allied use of local time or GMT ('Z') in logs.]
[Ed.

APX-004 United States Destroyers Escorting One Or More Westbound Convoys Between May 10 And December 7, 1941

USS KENDRICK	BENSON
USS MADISON	BENSON
USS MAYO	BENSON
USS DALLAS	CLEMSON
USS GREENE	CLEMSON
USS INGHAM	CLEMSON
USS MACLEISH	CLEMSON
USS McCORMICK	CLEMSON
USS OVERTON	CLEMSON
USS REUBEN JAMES	**CLEMSON**
USS SIMPSON	CLEMSON
USS STURTEVANT	CLEMSON
USS TRUXTUN	CLEMSON
USS BUCK	FLETCHER
USSMROE	FLETCHER

USS SPENCER	FLETCHER
USS EBERLE	GLEVES
USS EDISON	GLEVES
USS ERICSSON	GLEVES
USS GLEAVES	GLEVES
USS LEARY	GLEVES
USS LIVERMORE	GLEVES
USS LUDLOW	GLEVES
USS NIBLACK	GLEVES
USS NICHOLSON	GLEVES
USS PLUNKETT	GLEVES
USS BERNADOU	WICKES
USS COLE	WICKES
USS DICKERSON	WICKES
USS DUPONT	WICKES
USS ELLIS	WICKES
USS GREER	WICKES

USS HAMILTON	WICKES
USS HERBERT	WICKES
USS LANSDALE	WICKES
USS LEA	WICKES
USS ROPER	WICKES
USS SCHENCK	WICKES
USS TARBELL	WICKES
USS UPSHUR	WICKES
USS WOOLSEY	WICKES

Clemson and Wickes class were flush deck four-stack destroyers, all others of modern silhouette.

APX-005 Complete List Of Ships in Convoy HX-156 October, 1941

Ship	Registration
Alchiba	Dutch
Ancylus	British
Anna-Knudsen	Norway
Arabian-prince	British
Athelvictor	British
Benmacdhui	British
Britishabant	Belgium
Britishalant	Norway
British Governor	British
Cape-Britisheton	British
Charlbury	British
Chepo	Panama
Clan-Macquarrie	British
Comanchee	British

Delilian	British
Edam	Dutch
Eidanger	Norway
El-Capitan	Panama
El-Estero	Panama
Empire-Confidence	British
Empire-Day	British
Empire-Foam	British
Empire-Rainbow	British
Empire-Tern	British
Gallia	Norway
Ganymedes	Dutch
Knudsen	Norway
Leonatus	Panama
Lewant	Poland
Maihar	British
Markhor	British

Meldahl	Norway
Nestor	British
Norefjord	Norway
Polandar-Chief	British
Prince-De-Liege	Belgium
Prins-Willem-Van-Oranje	Dutch
San Alvaro	British
San-Emiliano	British
San-Rcadio	British
Sandanger	Norway
Skaraas	Norway
Sourabaya	British
Svanholm	British
Troubadour	Norway

APX-006 WARTIME LOG BOOK U-552
SIXTH PATROL
Kapitänleutnant Erich Topp
Period October 30,1941 – November 01, 1941
(Translation by Jerry Mason with the help of Ken Dunn and Rainer Kolbicz)

31.10.41

0400 AK 9982 *S 1-2, cloudy, bright moonlit night, Sea 1 Convoy sighted in the moonlit night at about 5 nm range. Large ships.*

0510 *Radio message: Convoy in sight AK 9973, enemy steering a northerly course, speed 10 knots U-552*

0556 *Radio message: Enemy position in square AK 9957, course 10°, speed 8 knots U-552*

0630 *Radio message:: Convoy in sight AK9951, course 30°, 9kts*

0708 *Initiated the attack after the moon has set. Although visibility is still too great due to aurora borealis and stars. Escorts are positioned far from the convoy, but are so numerous that in the short time available time before it gets light no way through is found.*

[ATTACK ON USS REUBEN JAMES]

0800 AK 9927 *Until 08.00 hours only encountered escort vessels.*
At 1000 meters a destroyer silhouette attacked and sunk with a two-fan. Both hit. High tongue of flame. Wreck is disintegrated by enormous detonation own depth charges.

0834 *Ran off a bit and could not start a new approach in time because of coming brightness.*

1010 *Met Endraß. Gave situation report by megaphone, after that both held contact on the port side.*

1059 *Radio message:: Square 9686 course 30° U-552*

1200 AK 9658 *SE 3, nearly overcast, Sea 2-3*
1214 *Radio message: AK 9667, Delta 20°, speed 9 knots U-552*
No difficulties with the contact report. Good visibility.
1330 *Radio message: AK9662, course 0° U-552*

APX-007 OFFICE OF THE CHIEF OF PATHOLOGY
UNITED STATES NAVAL SUPPORT FACILITY
CAMP TIEN SHA
DANANG R.V.N.

15 DEC 1966
Date.........
A-06-1105
Path #..............

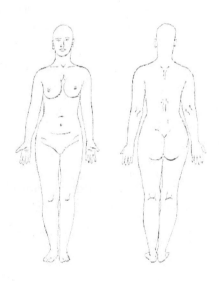

Name: REDACTED **DOB:** 13 Jun 1942 **S.N:** REDACTED **Gender:** F
Height: 65 Inches **Weight:** 125 Lbs **Race:** Caucasian **Blood Type:** B-
Hair: Brown **Eyes:** Green **Identifying Marks:** *Tattoos Pig, Left Ankle*
approx 2 inches square; Chicken, Right Ankle approx 2 inches square

OFFICE OF THE CHIEF OF PATHOLOGY
UNITED STATES NAVAL SUPPORT FACILITY
CAMP TIEN SHA
DANANG R.V.N.

15 December 1966
FROM: Howard M. St. George, Captain, MC, USN
TO: Chief of Surgery and Medicine, U.S. Seventh Fleet
Subject: Post Mortem Examination of: REDACTED

The remains of this twenty-six year old female was first presented to me upon my arrival at my laboratory at 0815 (Local), 13 December 1966. A representative of the Judge Advocate General's Corps and two enlisted representatives of the XXIV Corps Military Police Brigade, Danang accompanied the medical corpsmen.

A summary examination of the body disclosed a ligature around the neck. Also noted was a large area of abrasion or contusion in the pelvic area A prominent dried abrasion was present on the lower right buttock.

<u>External Evidence Of Injury:</u> Located just below the right ear at the right angle of the mandible, 1.5 inches below the right external auditory canal is a 3/8 x 1/4 inch area of rust colored abrasion. In the lateral aspect of the left lower eyelid on the inner conjunctival surface is a 1 mm in maximum dimension petechial hemorrhage. Relatively large, 4mm petechial

hemorrhages are present on the skin of the upper eyelids bilaterally as well as on the lateral left cheek. Possible petechial hemorrhages are also seen on the conjunctival surfaces of the right upper and lower eyelids, but liver mortis on this side of the face makes definite identification difficult.

A deep ligature furrow encircles the entire neck. The width of the furrow varies from one-eight of an inch to five/sixteenths of an inch and is horizontal in orientation, with little upward deviation. The skin of the anterior neck above and below the ligature furrow contains areas of petechial hemorrhage and abrasion encompassing an area measuring approximately 3 x 2 inches. The ligature furrow crosses the anterior midline of the neck just below the laryngeal prominence, approximately at the level of the cricoid cartilage. It is almost completely horizontal with slight upward deviation from the horizontal towards the back of the neck. The midline of the furrow mark on the anterior neck is 8 inches below the top of the head. The midline of the furrow mark on the posterior neck is 8.75 inches below the top of the head.

The area of abrasion and petechial hemorrhage of the skin of the anterior neck includes on the lower left neck, just to the left of the midline, a roughly triangular, parchment-like rust colored abrasion which measures 1.5 inches in length with a maximum width of 0.75 inches. This roughly triangular shaped abrasion is obliquely oriented with the apex superior and lateral. The remainder of the abrasions and petechial hemorrhages of the skin above and below the anterior projection of the ligature furrow are nonpatterned, purple to rust colored, and present in the midline, right, and left areas of the anterior neck. The skin just above the ligature furrow along the right side of the neck contains petechial hemorrhage composed of multiple confluent very small petechial hemorrhages as well as several larger petechial hemorrhages measuring up to one-sixteenth and one-eight of an inch in maximum dimension. Similar smaller petechial hemorrhages are present on the skin below the ligature furrow on the left lateral aspect of the neck. Located on the right side of the chin is a three-sixteenths by one-eight of an inch area of superficial abrasion. On the posterior aspect of the right shoulder is a poorly demarcated, very superficial focus of abrasion/contusion which is pale purple in color and measures up to three-quarters by one-half inch in maximum dimension. Several linear aggregates of petechial hemorrhages are present in the anterior left shoulder just above deltopectoral groove. These measure up to one inch in length by one-sixteenth to one-eight of an inch in width. On the left lateral aspect of the lower back, approximately sixteen and one-quarter inches and seventeen and one-half inches below the level of the top of the head are two dried rust colored to slightly purple abrasions. The more superior of the two measures one-eight by one-sixteenth of an inch and the more inferior measures three-sixteenths by one-eight of an inch. There is no surrounding contusion identified. On the posterior aspect of the left lower leg, almost in the midline, approximately 4 inches above the level of the heel are two large scratch-like abrasions which are dried and rust colored. They measure 2 inches by less than one-sixteenth of an inch and 4.4 inches by less than one-sixteenth of an inch respectively.

On the anterior aspect of the perineum, along the edges of closure of the labia majora, is a very large amount of dried blood. A smaller amount of dried and semi-fluid blood is present on the skin of the fourchette and in the vestibule. Inside the vestibule of the vagina and along the distal vaginal wall is reddish hyperemia. This hyperemia is circumferential and is much more noticeable on the right side and posteriorly. The hyperemia also appears to extend just inside the vaginal orifice. Vestigial hymen tissue is represented by a rim of mucosal tissue extending clockwise between the 2 and 10:00 positions. On the right labia majora is a very large area of violent discoloration measuring approximately two inches by two and one half inch. Incision into the underlying subcutaneous tissue discloses significant hemorrhage. A large amount of seminal fluid is present in the vaginal vault. Significant anal and other perineal trauma is identified.

Remainder Of External Examination: The unembalmed, well developed and well nourished Caucasian female body measures 64 inches in length and weights an estimated 112 pounds.

No scalp trauma is identified. The external auditory canals are patent and free of blood. The eyes are green and the pupils equally dilated. The sclerae are white. The nostrils are both patent and contain a small amount of tan mucous material. The teeth are native and in good repair and a list of restorations has been compiled for comparison to USN dental records, The tongue is smooth, pink-tan and granular. No buccal mucosal trauma is seen. The frenulum is intact. There is slight drying artifact of the tip of the tongue. On the right cheek is a pattern of dried saliva and mucous material which appears to be hemorrhagic. The neck contains no palpable adenopathy or masses and the trachea and larynx are midline. The chest is symmetrical. Breasts are bruised and prominent.. The abdomen is flat and contains scar tissue indicating appendectomy at some undefined date. No palpable organomegaly or masses are identified. The external genitalia are that of a mature female. Very short pubic hair is present. The anus is distended. Examination of the extremities indicate a tattoo of a pig on the anterior of the right ankle, and a similarly sized tattoo of a chicken of the left ankle.

The fingernails of both hands are of sufficient length for clipping. Examination of the back is unremarkable. Scrapings indicate skin from a Caucasian or Caucasians. There is dorsal 3+ to 4+ livor mortis which is nonblanching. Livor mortis is also present on the right side of the face. At the time of the initiation of the autopsy there is mild 1 to 2+ rigor mortis of the elbows and shoulders with more advanced 2 to 3+ rigor mortis of the joints of the lower extremities.

Internal Exam: The anterior chest musculature is well developed. No sternal or rib fractures are identified.

Mediastinum: The mediastinal contents are normally distributed. The thymus gland has a normal external appearance. The cut sections are finely lobular and pink-tan. No petechial hemorrhages are seen. The aorta and remainder of the mediastinal structures are unremarkable.

Body Cavities: The right and left thoracic cavities contain approximately 25 cc of straw colored fluid. The pleural surfaces are smooth and glistening. The pericardial sac contains 3-4 cc of straw colored fluid and the epicardium and pericardium are unremarkable. The abdominal contents are normally distributed and covered by a smooth glistening serosa. No intra-abdominal accumulation of fluid or blood is seen.

Lungs: The right lung and left lung have a normal lobar configuration. An occasional scattered subpleural petechial hemorrhage is seen on the surface of each lung. The cut sections of the lungs disclose an intact alveolar architecture with a small amount of watery fluid exuding from the cut surfaces with mild pressure. The intrapulmonary bronchi and vasculature are unremarkable. No evidence of consolidation is seen.

Heart: The 1 heart has a normal external configuration. There are scattered subepicardial petechial hemorrhages over the anterior surface of the heart. The coronary arteries are normal in their distribution and contain no evidence of atherosclerosis. The tan- pink myocardium is homogeneous and contains no areas of fibrosis or infarction. The endocardium is unremarkable. The valve cusps are thin, delicate and pliable and contain no vegetation or thrombosis. The major vessels enter and leave the heart in the normal fashion. The foramen ovale is closed.

Aorta and Vena Cava: The aorta is patent throughout its course as are its major branches. No atherosclerosis is seen. The Vena Cava is unremarkable.

Spleen: The spleen has a finely wrinkled purple capsule. Cut sections are homogeneous and disclose readily identifiable red and white pulp. No intrinsic abnormalities are identified.

Adrenals: The adrenal glands are of normal size and shape. A golden yellow cortex surmounts a thin brown-tan medullary area. No intrinsic abnormalities are identified.

Kidneys: The right kidney and left kidney have a normal external appearance. The surfaces are smooth and glistening. Cut sections disclose an intact corticomedullary architecture. The renal papilae are sharply demarcated. The pelvocaliceal system is lined by gray-white mucosa which is unremarkable. Both ureters are patent throughout their course to the bladder.

Liver: The liver has a normal external appearance. The capsule is smooth and glistening. Cut sections disclose an intact lobular architecture with no intrinsic abnormalities identified.

Pancreas: The pancreas is of normal size and shape. Cut sections are finely lobular and tan. No intrinsic abnormalities are identified.

Bladder: The bladder is contracted and contains no urine. The bladder mucosa is smooth and tan-gray. No intrinsic abnormalities are seen.

Genitalia: The upper portions of the vaginal vault contain is severely bruised. The uterus is unremarkable. The cervical contains no abnormalities. Both fallopian tubes and ovaries are unremarkable by gross examination.

Gallbladder: The gallbladder contains 2-3 cc of amber bile. No stones are identified and the mucosa is smooth and velvety. The cystic duct, right and left hepatic duct and common bile duct are patent throughout their course to the duodenum.

G.I. Tract: The esophagus is empty. It is lined by gray-white mucosa. The stomach contains a small amount (8-10 cc) of viscous to green to tan colored thick mucous material without particulate matter identified. The gastric mucosa is autolyzed but contains no areas of hemorrhage or ulceration. The proximal portion of the small intestine contains fragmented pieces of yellow to light green-tan apparent vegetable or fruit material which may represent fragments of pineapple. No hemorrhage is identified. The remainder of the small intestine is unremarkable. The large intestine contains soft green fecal material. The appendix is not present.

Lymphatic System: Unremarkable.

Musculoskeletal System: Unremarkable.

Skull and Brain: Upon reflection of the scalp there is found to be an extensive area of scalp hemorrhage along the right temporoparietal area extending from the orbital ridge, posteriorly all the way to the occipital area. This encompasses an area measuring approximately 7 x 4 inches. This grossly appears to be fresh hemorrhage with no evidence of organization. At the superior extension of this area of hemorrhage is a linear to comminuted skull fracture which extends from the right occipital to posteroparietal area forward to the right frontal area across the parietal portion of the skull. the posteroparietal area of this fracture is a roughly rectangular shaped displaced fragment of skull measuring one and three-quarters by one-half inch. The hemorrhage and the fracture extend posteriorly just past the midline of the occipital area of the skull. This fracture measures approximately 8.5 inches in length. On removal of the skull cap there is found to be a thin film of subdural hemorrhage measuring approximately 7-8 cc over the surface of the right cerebral hemisphere and extending to the base of the cerebral hemisphere. The

1450 gm brain has a normal overall architecture. Mild narrowing of the sulci and flattening of the gyri are seen. No inflammation is identified. There is a thin film of subarachnoid hemorrhage overlying the entire right cerebral hemisphere. On the right cerebral hemisphere underlying the previously mentioned linear skull fracture is an extensive linear area of purple contusion extending from the right frontal area, posteriorly along the lateral aspect of the parietal region and into the occipital area. This area of contusion measures 8 inches in length with a width of up to 1.75 inches. At the tip of the right temporal lobe is a one-quarter by one quarter inch similar appearing purple contusion. Only very minimal contusion is present at the tip of the left temporal lobe. This area of contusion measures only one-half inch in maximum dimension. The cerebral vasculature contains no evidence of atherosclerosis. Multiple coronal sections of the cerebral hemispheres, brain stem and cerebullum disclose no additional abnormalities. The areas of previously described contusion are characterized by purple linear streak-like discolorations of the gray matter perpendicular to the surface of the cerebral cortex. These extend approximately 6 mm into the cerebral cortex. Examination of the base of the brain discloses no additional fractures.

Neck: Dissection of the neck is performed after removal of the thoracoabdominal organs and the brain. The anterior strap musculature of the neck is serially dissected. Multiple sections of the sternocleidomastoid muscle disclose no hemorrhages. Sections of the remainder of the strap musculature of the neck disclose no evidence of hemorrhage. Examination of the thyroid cartilage, cricoid cartilage and hyoid bone disclose not evidence of fracture of hemorrhage. Multiple cross sections of the tongue disclose no hemorrhage or traumatic injury. The thyroid gland is normal in appearance. Cut sections are finely lobular and red-tan. The trachea and larynx are lined by smooth pink-tan mucosa without intrinsic abnormalities.

Microscopic Description: (All Sections Stained with H&E)

(Slide Key) - (A) - scalp hemorrhage, (B) - sections of vaginal mucosa with smallest fragment representing area of abrasion of 7:00 position, (C) - heart, (D-F) - lungs, (G) - liver and spleen, (H) - pancreas and kidney, (I) - thyroid and bladder, (J) - thymus and adrenals, (K-L) - reproductive organs, (M) - larynx, (N-T) - brain.

Myocardium: Sections of the ventricular myocardium are composed of interlacing bundles of cardiac muscle fibers. No fibrosis or inflammation are identified.

Lungs: The alveolar architecture of the lungs is well preserved. Pulmonary vascular congestion is identified. No intrinsic abnormalities are seen.

Spleen: There is mild autolysis of the spleen. Both red and white pulp are identifiable.

Thyroid: The thyroid gland is composed of normal-appearing follicles. An occasional isolated area of chronic interstitial inflammatory infiltrate is seen. There is also a small fragment of parathyroid tissue.

Thymus: The thymus gland retains the usual architecture. The lymphoid material is intact and scattered Hassall's corpuscles are identified. Mild vascular congestion is identified.

Trachea: There is mild chronic inflammation in the submucosa of the trachea.

Liver: The lobular architecture of the liver is well preserved. No inflammation or intrinsic abnormality are identified.

Pancreas: There is autolysis of the pancreas which is otherwise unremarkable.

Kidney: The overall architecture of the kidney is well preserved. There is perhaps mild vascular congestion in the cortex but no inflammation is identified.

Bladder: The transitional epithelium of the bladder is autolyzed. No significant intrinsic abnormalities are seen.

Reproductive Organs: Sections of the uterus are consistent with the the stated age. The ovary is unremarkable.

Adrenal: The architecture of the adrenal is well preserved and no intrinsic abnormalities are seen.

Brain: Sections of the areas of contusion disclose disrupted blood vessels of the cortex with surrounding hemorrhage. There is no evidence of inflammatory infiltrate or organization of the hemorrhage. Subarachnoid hemorrhage is also identified. Cortical neurons are surrounded by clear halos, as are glial cells.

Vaginal Mucosa: All of the sections contain vascular congestion and focal interstitial chronic inflammation. the smallest piece of tissue, from the 7:00 position of the vaginal wall/hymen, contain epithelial erosion with underlying capillary congestion. A large number of red blood cells is present on the eroded surface, as is semen and birefringent foreign material. Acute inflammatory infiltrate is not seen.

Evidence: Items turned over to the Judge Advocates Corps as evidence include: Fibers and hair from clothing and body surfaces; ligatures; clothing; vaginal swabs and smears; rectal swabs and smears; oral swabs and smears; paper bags from hands, fingernail clippings, jewelry, paper bags from feet; camouflaged body bag; sample of head hair, eyelashes and eyebrows; swabs from right and left thighs and right cheek; red top and purple top tubes of blood.

Addendum: At 1125 (Local) this date, at my request Ljtg. Walter Cox, MC, USN joined me in the examination under my direct supervision. Dr. Cox documented more than one hundred twenty-five bruises, many of which he identified as acute injures that had been inflicted within a few hours of death. The bruising indicated that this female had been severely beaten about her head, face, upper and lower torso, arms, legs, and genitalia. He also detailed that the blows to her abdomen had resulted in severe internal trauma, including hemorrhaging in her stomach, intestine and other internal organs. Dr. Cox concluded that death occurred as a result of cardiovascular collapse stemming from the severe, blunt force trauma to her abdomen, and the numerous related complications. He also discovered during the autopsy additional evidence of acute anal penetration. Based upon the presence of contusions and lacerations, Dr. Cox determined that this female had sustained repetitive anal and vaginal penetrations over a period of time, and that the most recent anal trauma had occurred sometime during the past twelve hours. Given the prominence of abrasions within the rectum, Dr. Cox further concluded that this female had been anally and vaginally penetrated by a penis or penises, as well as a finger or some other foreign object, and death was caused by vaginal and anal causing *exsanguination* over a course of several hours, as well as suffocation caused by ligature as outlined above.

FINAL DIAGNOSIS:

A. Ligature strangulation

B. *Exsanguination* From Lacerations Of Anus And Pelvis

C. Circumferential ligature with associated ligature furrow of neck

D. Abrasions and petechial hemorrhages, neck

E. Petechial hemorrhages, conjunctival surfaces of eyes and skin of face

II. Craniocerebral Injuries

A. Scalp contusion

B. Linear, comminuted fracture of right side of skull

C. Linear pattern of contusions of right cerebral hemisphere

D. subarachnoid and subdural hemorrhage
E. Small contusions, tips of temporal lobes
F.. Abrasion of right cheek
G.. Abrasion/contusion, posterior right shoulder
H. Abrasions of left lower back and posterior left lower leg
I. Abrasion and vancular congestion of vaginal mucosa

<u>Toxicologic Studies:</u>

Blood Ethanol - None Detected
Blood Drug Screen - No Drugs Detected

> ***<u>Clinocopatholigical Correlation:</u> Cause of death of this twenty-six year old female is asphyxia by strangulation associated with craniocerebral trauma, and*** exsanguination ***caused by severe trauma to vagina and rectum.***

GLOSSARY

'ANGASHORE – Person who never goes to sea. (Newfoundland)

BINNICLE LIST – List of sailors unfit for duty due to illness or injury

CAM RANH BAY – Port on coast of Vietnam, about 300 km north of Saigon

COMMAND DUTY OFFICER- Officer delegated authority in absence of the C.O.

DANANG- Port on the north-central coast of Vietnam, about 950 km north of Saigon

MOMP - Mid-Ocean Meeting Point, transfer point for convoy escorts

SERGEANT MAJOR OF THE MARINE CORPS -Senior Enlisted member of entire USMC

AIR AMERICA – CIA's proprietary air service during the Vietnam war.

ARVN – Army Of The Republic Of Vietnam

BOATSWAIN – In USMM usage, senior unlicensed mariner and deck-crew foreman.

BROW – A movable bridge used in boarding or leaving a ship at a pier or wharf.

BUNDESMARINE-- Seagoing arm of defense forces of Federal Republic of Germany.

CAMP TIEN SHA – Base to west of Monkey Mountain (Núi Sơn Trà in Vietnamese)

CENTER CITY – Local appellation for the downtown area of Philadelphia

CHIEF YEOMAN –A senior administrative specialist in USN and USCG.

CONUS – Continental United States.

DEROS-- Date Of Expected Return From Oversea Service

DONKEYMAN – Unlicensed mariner responsible for secondary engines, i.e windless etc.

FRG-- Federal Republic of Germany before re-unification

JOOD – Junior Officer of the Deck. Assists the OOD and CDO in their duties.

GLOSSARY

MASTER CHIEF PETTY OFFICER OF THE NAVY-- -Senior Enlisted member of entire USN

MEDCAPS – Medical Civic Action Program; medical assistance to local populations

MSTS-- Military Sea Transportation Service, inter alia, contracts with civilian shipping

NMU-- National Maritime Union. Woody Gutherie was a proud and vocal member.

PLIMSOLL LINE – The painted scale which marks safe loading depth under various conditions.

RITTENHOUSE SQ, –Very upscale residence/shopping area at 18 & Walnut, Philadelphia

ROUNDHOUSE-- Philadelphia iconic Police Administration Building at 8th & Race Street

RVN – Republic of Vietnam.

SEPTA--- Southeast Pennsylvania Transit Authority.

SWALLOWING THE ANCHOR-- Sailor's term for retirement

TAD – Temporary Assignment for Duty, usually 90 days or less.

USS SANCTUARY (AH-17) – USN hospital ship of the Haven class active in Vietnam

VICE ADMIRAL – Senior Naval officer, ranks between Rear Admiral (UH) and Admiral.

WHITE ELEPHANT–Naval Support Activity Danang HQ near the Han River

Y" GUN.-- Depth charge launching mechanism before & during WW-II.

ONLINE RESOURCES AND NOTES

1. The address presented by Rear Admiral Erich Topp was adapted and abridged from the preface of his autobiography: The Odyssey Of A U-Boat Commander: Recollections of Erich Topp, Westport, CT: Praeger Publications, *under Fair Use provisions of 17USC-107, as amended, and comprises less than 0.5% of the original work.*

2. The Escort Reports quoted verbatim in Chapter 10 may be viewed in their original state: http://www.fold3.com/browse.php#1hsEUS91acSoo I8J03Gjg48D6uoCE7EPk9

3. Crew List US Reuben James:
http://www.warsailors.com/convoys/hxescorts.html retrieved 19 Aug 2014

4. Clemson-Class Destroyers to UK:
http://www.history.navy.mil/research/library/online-reading-room/title-list- alphabetically/d/destroyers transferred-to-britain-under-destroyers-for-bases-agreement.html retrieved 14 Oct 2014

5. Nautical Almanac for 31 Oct 41:
http://www.uboatarchive.net/U-552/KTB552-6NO-31-10-41.htm retrieved 23 Jul 2014

6. N. Atlantic U.S. Destroyers: May-Dec.41: http://www.warsailors.com/convoys/hxescorts.html
retrieved 12 Aug 2014

7. Roster, Convoy HX-156 in October 1941:
http://www.warsailors.com/convoys/hx156.html
retrieved 22 May 2014

8. Excerpts of Deck Log U-552 for 31 Oct 41   http://www.uboatarchive.net/KTB552-6.htm
retrieved 11Dec 2014. [thanks, Captain Jerry Mason for the tip!]

9. New York Times articles quoted in Chapter 12 – NYT ONLINE ARCHIVES:
h t t p : / / q u e r y . n y t i m e s . c o m / s e a r c h / s i t e s e a r c h / # / REUBEN+JAMES+SINKING/

- *(a.)November 01, 1941 - By CHARLES HERD - Print Headline: "REUBEN JAMES HIT; First American Warship Lost in War Torpedoed West of Iceland"*
- *(b.)November 01, 1941 - By JAMES B. RESTON - Print Headline: "SINKING QUICKENS CONGRESS ACTION; Members' Comment Indicates Drastic Neutrality Law Revision Is Expedited"*
- *(c.)November 25, 1941 - - Print Headline: "MEN DESCRIBE LOSS OF REUBEN JAMES; One Petty Officer Left Led 44 Surviving Enlisted Men to the Rescue Rafts*

NOTE:*The Autopsy Report for LTJG Mary Kay Carpentier NC, USNR, alluded to in Chapter 17 and contained in appendix seven, is like the character herself, completely fictitious.*

OTHER READINGS

The reader may be interested in these works, which present the significant events of 1940-1941 without the overlay of fiction.

Abbazia, P, (1975) **Mr. Roosevelt's Navy: Private War of the United States Atlantic Fleet, 1939-42,** 1st ed. Annapolis, Md: Naval Institute Press.

Blair C., (1996). ***Hitler's U-Boat War.*** 1st ed. New York: Random House.

Hagan J. and Leahy J., (2006) ***The Chief Petty Officer's Guide.*** 1st ed. Annapolis, MD: Naval Institute Press

Henrichs, W., (1988). ***Threshold of War: Franklin Roosevelt and American Entry into World War II.*** 1st ed. Oxford U.K.: Oxford University Press

Mallmann Showell J.P., (2003). ***German Naval Code Breakers.*** 1st ed. Annapolis, MD: Naval Institute Press

Milner M., (1994). ***The U-Boat Hunters: The Royal Canadian Navy and the Offensive against Germany's Submarines.*** 1st ed. Toronto: University of Toronto Press.

Persico J, E., (2002). *Roosevelt's Secret War.* 1st ed. New York: Random House.

Topp, E. and Rust, E (ed), (1992) **The Odyssey Of A U-Boat Commander: Recollections of Erich Topp,** 1st ed. Westport, CT: Praeger Publications

Wilson T.A., (1991). *The First Summit: Roosevelt and Churchill at Placentia Bay, 1941.* 2nd ed. Lawrence KS: University Press of Kansas.

OTHER BOOKS BY MR LEAHY:

Come From Away: The Plot to Assassinate Churchill – 1941 (Naval Writers Group, Annapolis MD, 2013) ISBN-13: 978-0615669625

Lost at Sea–An Enlisted Woman's Journey (with Rebecca Anne Freeman). (Naval Writers Group, Annapolis MD, 2005) ISBN-13: 978-1595260956

The Chief Petty Officer's Guide. (With John Hagan) (Naval Institute Press, Annapolis, Maryland, 2004). ISBN-13: 978-1591144595

Ask The Chief – Backbone of the Navy (Naval Institute Press, Annapolis, Maryland, 2004) ISBN-13: 978-1591144410

Honor, Courage, Commitment – Navy Boot Camp (Naval Institute Press, Annapolis, Maryland, 2002); ISBN-13: 978-1591144380

Further information about these books may be found at
www.navalwritersgroup.us

ABOUT THE AUTHOR

J.F. (Jack) Leahy is a noted writer on naval topics, and is the author of six books on the subject. After completing his undergraduate studies, he served with Mobile Construction Battalion One at Phu Bai and Danang Vietnam in 1969-70. After completing his graduate education as a civilian, he spent nearly thirty years in the intelligence community and telecommunications industry. Upon retiring in 2000, he first taught at Franklin University in Columbus, Ohio. In 2011, he retired as Vice President for Strategic Planning and Extension Services of the Pontifical College Josephinum, a Roman Catholic seminary also in Columbus, Ohio, where he resides with his wife, Margaret.

ABOUT THE PUBLISHER

Established by a cadre of writers who first met through the Naval Institute at the Naval Academy, Annapolis in 2002, the Naval Writers Group is a specialized publishing imprint which provides a voice to "the sailor on the deck plates." No distinction is ever made based upon the author's rating or rank – be it seaman or admiral – for we strongly believe that each story deserves to be evaluated on its merit alone. You may learn more about the Naval Writers Group at www.navalwritersgroup.us or by contacting exdir@navalwritersgroup.us.

IN LOVING MEMORY:

RITA E. FRANKENSTEIN
1919 - 1999